항공 승무원을 위한

항공 객실 서비스 영어

AIRCRAFT CABIN SERVICE ENGLISH

Based on NCS

NCS 기반

항공객실 서비스영어

Preface
머리말

    항공실무영어와 관련된 다양한 교재가 이미 출간되어 사용되고 있습니다. 기존의 교재들과 비교하여 본 교재의 차별화된 특징 중 하나는 NCS에 기반한 국내 최초의 항공객실서비스 영어 교재라는 점입니다. 국가는 산업현장의 요구에 부응하고, 현장중심의 실무능력을 갖춘 인재양성을 목표로 국가직무능력표준 (National Competency Standards)을 개발하였습니다. 직무명 '항공객실서비스'는 24개의 대분류 중 열두 번째 '숙박여행·오락', 4개의 중분류 중 세 번째 '관광·레저', 4개의 소분류 중 첫 번째 '여행서비스'에 속해 있으며 5개의 세분류 중 다섯 번째인 '항공객실서비스'를 바탕으로 구축되었습니다.

    세분류 '항공객실서비스'의 모듈이 개발되어 항공객실 서비스실무와 관련된 국가 차원의 체계적인 교육의 기틀을 마련하였으나 이를 영어로 교육할 교재는 부재한 상태입니다. 이에 본 집필진은 그 동안에 쌓아온 영어교육 및 항공객실 서비스교육의 경험과 전문성을 바탕으로 NCS기반 항공객실서비스영어 교재를 제작하게 되었습니다. 최초의 시도임으로 내용 및 구성 상 부족함이 존재하지만 앞으로 본 교재를 발판으로 보다 발전된 항공객실서비스영어 교재가 지속적으로 제작되기를 희망합니다.

    본 교재는 크게 2개의 Part로 구성되었으며 Part 1은 항공객실서비스 (Cabin Service)를, Part 2는 항공안전 (Flight Safety)을 다루고 있습니다. Part 1은 10

개의 Unit으로 구성되어 있는데 이는 NCS의 세분류 '항공객실서비스'의 14개의 능력단위 중 7개 능력단위를 포함하고 있으며 이륙 전 서비스, 비행 중 서비스, 착륙 전 서비스, 착륙 후 서비스, 객실승무 관리 등을 다루고 있습니다. Part 2 항공 안전은 2개의 Unit으로 구성되어 있으며 2개의 능력단위, '기내 안전관리'와 '응급환자 대처'를 다루고 있습니다. 각각의 Unit은 학습목표 (Objective Duties), 어휘와 어구 (Words and Phrases), 대화 (Dialogue), 응용대화 (Substitution Drill), 추가정보 (Additional Information)로 구성되어 있습니다.

국제적인 업무라 할 수 있는 항공객실 서비스실무는 전문지식과 정보의 습득을 요구할 뿐 아니라 세련되고 수준 높은 영어실력을 필수적으로 요구하고 있습니다. 각 Unit에 포함된 능력단위요소와 관련된 상황에서의 원활한 영어소통 능력 향상을 위해 기본 대화 제시에 이어 응용대화 연습의 기회도 제공하였습니다. 다양하고 깊이 있는 실전에 강한 영어어휘 및 표현을 다루고 있어 국내 항공사와 더불어 외국 항공사 취업준비에 도움을 주고자 하였습니다. 항공실무와 관련된 추가정보를 제공하였으므로 교수자는 학습자의 수준과 요구에 따라 탄력적으로 취사선택하여 교육할 수 있습니다.

현 항공업계는 객실 내 승객뿐 아니라 동료 승무원, 지상직 요원, 기타 항공 관련 요원들과의 원활한 영어소통 능력이 요구되는 명실상부한 국제적인 비즈니스의 무대입니다. 아무쪼록 업계가 요구하는 준비된 승무원양성, 면접과 실무에 강한 인재양성을 위해 본 교재가 활용되기를 희망합니다. 끝으로 본 책이 나오기 까지 응원해 주시고 지원해 주신 동료교수님들께 깊은 감사의 뜻을 전하며, 감수에 시간을 아끼지 않았던 James Forscutt 선생님께도 진심 어린 감사의 마음을 전합니다.

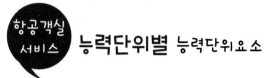

항공객실 서비스 능력단위별 능력단위요소

분류번호	능력단위	수준	능력단위요소
1203010501_15v2	기내 안전관리	3	승객 탑승 전 안전 · 보안 점검하기
			항공기 이 · 착륙전 안전 · 보안 관리하기
			비행 중 안전 · 보안 관리하기
			착륙 후 안전 · 보안 점검 · 관리
			비상사태 발생 시 대응하기
			상황별 안전안내 방송하기
1203010502_13v1	승객 탑승 전 준비	3	기내서비스용품 점검하기
			서비스 설비 및 기물 점검하기
			특별 서비스 요청사항 점검하기
1203010503_16v2	승객 탑승 및 이륙 전 서비스	3	탑승위치 대기하기
			탑승권 재확인하기
			좌석 안내하기
			수하물 정리 지원하기
			특수 고객 지원하기
1203010504_13v1	비행 중 서비스	3	기내음료 제공하기
			기내식 제공하기
			기내 오락물 제공하기
			면세품 판매하기
			객실 상태 점검하기
1203010505_16v2	착륙 전 서비스	3	입국 서류 배포 및 작성 지원하기
			기내 용품 회수하기
			기내 서비스용품 및 면세품 재고 확인하기
1203010506_16v2	착륙 후 서비스	3	승객 하기 지원하기
			특수 고객 지원하기

분류번호	능력단위	수준	능력단위요소
1203010507_13v1	승객 하기 후 관리	3	유실물 점검하기
			잔류 승객 점검하기
			기내 설비 점검하기
			기내 용품 인수 · 인계하기
1203010508_13v1	응급환자 대처	3	응급환자 발생상황 파악 · 보고하기
			응급환자 초기 대응하기
			응급환자 후속 관리하기
			환자 대처 상황 기록하기
1203010509_16v2	객실승무 관리	4	객실 승무원별 근무 배정하기
			운항 · 객실간 정보 공유하기
			불만 승객 관리하기
			출 · 도착 서류 작성 · 관리하기
			객실서비스 관리하기
1203010510_16v1	기내음료 서비스	2	기내음료 파악하기
			기내음료 제공하기
1203010511_16v1	항공서비스 업무 기본	2	항공서비스 관련 서류 확인하기
			항공여객정보 확인하기
1203010512_16v1	항공 기내방송 업무	3	항공기내 방송 준비하기
			정상적 상황 방송하기
			비정상 상황 방송하기
			비상 상황 방송하기
1203010513_16v1	고객만족 서비스	3	서비스 마인드 함양하기
			이미지 메이킹하기
			불만고객 대처하기
1203010514_16v1	항공서비스 매너	2	기본 매너 갖추기
			항공서비스 매너 관리하기

Contents
차례

Part 01

Cabin Service
항공 객실 서비스

Contents

Part
O2

Flight Safety
항공 안전

NCS기반
항공객실서비스영어

책의 특징

1) 국내 최초 NCS 세분류 '항공객실서비스' 기반 항공객실서비스영어 교재

2) NCS에 기반한 항공실무지식 습득을 위한 체계적 내용

3) 항공객실 서비스 업무와 관련된 수행준거를 바탕으로 영어어휘와 어구, 영어 대화연습, 그 밖의 추가 정보 제공

4) 승무원면접시험 및 실전업무 대비 단계별 교육내용

5) 응용대화(Substitution Drills)연습을 통한 다양한 상황에서 요구되는 영어능력 향상을 목표로 구성

6) 항공실무와 관련된 다양하고 깊이 있는 실전에 강한 영어어휘 및 표현 활용 및 습득을 목표로 구성

Cabin Service
항공 객실 서비스

Preparation for Boarding
승객 탑승 전 준비

---

1) Checking In-flight Service Items (기내 서비스 용품 점검하기)

 Objective Duties (학습 목표)

1. 운송 서비스 규정에 따라, 객실 서비스에 필요한 서비스 용품 탑재 여부를 점검하고 조치할 수 있다.

2. 운송 서비스 규정에 따라, 서비스 용품의 품질 상태 및 이상 유무를 점검하여, 조치할 수 있다.

3. 객실 서비스 규정에 따라, 서비스용품을 지정된 서비스 위치에 배열할 수 있다.

1. in-flight service items 기내 서비스 용품

2. interphone 인터폰, 실내전화, 비행기내 통화장치

3. first class(F/C) 일등석

4. business class(B/C) 비즈니스석

5. economy class(E/Y 또는 Y/C) 일반석

6. vegetable meal(VGML) 야채식

7. child meal(CHML) 어린이식

8. request 요청, 요구

9. loaded 탑재된

10. miss 없다, 놓치다

11. paper towel 종이 타올

12. staff 직원

13. catering service 음식공급(캐이터링) 서비스

14. Hindu meal(HNML) 힌두교식

15. Muslim meal(MOML) 이슬람교식

16. earphone 이어폰, 수신기

17. Kosher meal(KSML) 유태교식

18. Diabetic meal(DBML) 당뇨환자식

19. toothbrush 칫솔

20. Low-fat meal(LFML) 저지방식

21. Gluten intolerant meal(GFML) 저(무)글루텐식

22. seltzer 탄산수

Picture 1 — Cabin Service Items
& Cabin Service Check

Dialogue 1-1   Track ∘01

Checking the number of passengers and service items on the interphone.

> M : Cabin Manager   A1 : Flight Attendant 1
> A2 : Flight Attendant 2   A3 : Flight Attendant 3

M : Today, we have five first class (F/C) passengers, 23 business class (B/C) passengers, and 230 economy class (E/Y or Y/C) passengers. We have five vegetable meals (VGML) and two child meals (CHML) requests in economy class. Please make sure they're loaded when you check the service items.

A1 : Everything is fine in first class.

A2 : In business class we're missing paper towels and newspapers.

A3 : One child meal for the second meal service has not been loaded for economy class.

M : OK. ... (after a while) ... I've talked to the staff from the catering service. Once the child meal has been loaded, please let me know.

Substitution Drill 1-1

Direction : Practice the conversation with your partner using the information given in the table below.

M : Today, we have (1) _____ first class (F/C) passengers, _____ business class (B/C) passengers, and _____ economy class (E/Y or Y/C) passengers. We have (2) _____ requests in economy class. Please make sure they're loaded when you check the service items.

A1 : Everything is fine in first class.

A2 : In business class we're missing (3) _____ .

A3 : (4) _____ for the second meal service has not been loaded for economy class.

M : OK. ... (after a while) ... I've talked to the staff from the catering service. Once the (4) _____ has/have been loaded, please let me know.

	(1) Nuber of passengers	(2) Special meals requested	(3) Service items not loaded	(4) Special meal(s) not loaded
A	2, 21, 250	2 Hindu meals (HNML) and 3 Muslim meals (MOML)	earphones and napkins	1 Muslim meal
B	7, 26, 310	1 kosher meal (KSML) and 3 diabetic meals (DBML)	toothbrushes	1 Diabetic meal
C	2, 12, 189	2 low-fat meal (LFML) and 3 gluten intolerant meal (GFML)	Coke and seltzers	2 Gluten intolerant meals

2) Checking Service Facilities and Equipment
(서비스 설비 및 기물 점검하기)

Objective Duties (학습 목표)

1. 객실 서비스 규정에 따라 항공기 운항 시 반드시 필요한 서비스 설비 및 기물의 이상 여부를 점검하고 조치할 수 있다.
2. 객실 서비스 규정에 따라 항공기 운항 시 반드시 필요한 화장실 설비의 이상 유무를 점검하고 조치할 수 있다.
3. 운송 서비스 규정에 따라 항공기의 목적지 도착 시, 입국에 필요한 제반 입국 관련 서류의 탑재 여부 및 수량을 점검하고 조치할 수 있다.
4. 객실 서비스 규정에 따라 항공기 운항 시 판매할 면세품의 탑재 여부 및 수량을 점검하고 조치할 수 있다.

Words and Phrases (어휘와 어구)

Picture 2 — Oven

Picture 3 — Coffee Maker

Picture 4 — Water Boiler

1. facility 시설
2. equipment 장비
3. oven 오븐
4. coffee maker 커피 메이커, 커피 끓이는 기구

5. water boiler 물 끓이개

6. elevator 엘리베이터

7. garbage compressor 쓰레기 압축기

8. waste carton box 쓰레기 압축 종이상자

9. Audio & Video on Demand(AVOD)
   주문형 오디오 비디오 시스템

10. flight information 비행 정보

11. temperature indicator 온도 지시계

12. smoke detector 연기 탐지기

13. layout 레이아웃(배치)

14. upper deck 위층 갑판

15. lower deck 아래층 갑판

16. departure and arrival cards 출발 및
    도착 카드(신고서)

17. customs card 세관신고 카드(신고서)

18. duty-free item 면세 품목

19. via 경유하여, 거쳐서

20. mid-galley 중간 주방(조리실)

21. copy 알았다(기내 인터폰 또는 워키토키 등에서 사용)

22. once ~할 때

23. main deck galley 주 갑판 주방

24. out of order 고장 난

25. refrigerator 냉장고

26. lavatory 화장실

27. replace 대체하다

28. liquid 액체

29. fire extinguisher 소화기

30. filled with ~로 채워지다

Picture 5 — Elevator

Picture 6 — Garbage Compressor & Waste Carton Box

Picture 7 — Audio & Video on Demand

Picture 8 — Flight Information

Picture 9 — Temperature Indicator

Picture 10 — Smoke Detector

Picture 11 — Layout of an Aircraft

31. customs declaration form 세관 신고서

32. immigration form 출입국 신고서

33. CIQ(Customs, Immigration, and Quarantine) forms 세관, 출입국, 검역 신고서

34. catering personnel 음식공급업체 직원

35. seal number 봉인 넘버

36. POS system 판매유통시스템(판매 즉시 품목, 가격, 수량 등의 정보를 입력하고 분석할 수 있는 시스템)

37. quantity 양, 수량

38. essence 에센스(화장품의 일종), 본질, 진수

39. eau de toilette 수분이 많고 향이 강하지 않은 향수의 일종

Picture 12 — Lower Deck of an Airbus 380-800(407)

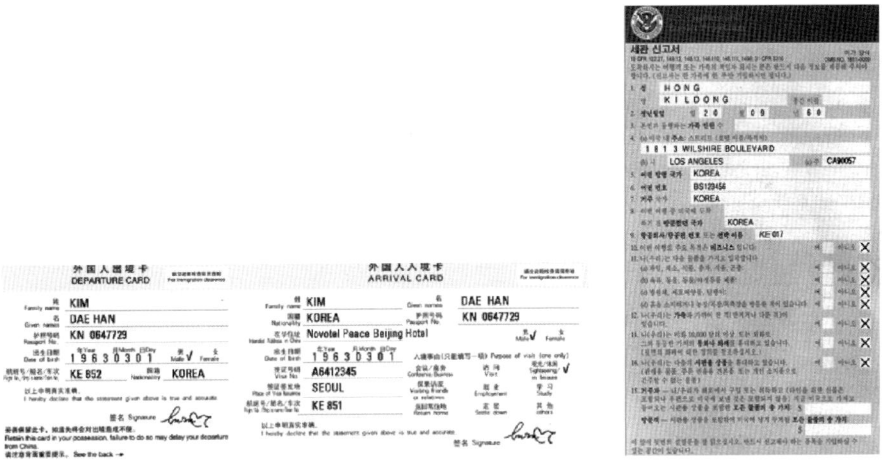

Picture 13 — Upper Deck of an Airbus 380-800(407)

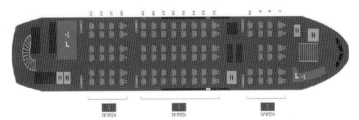

Picture 14 — Chinese Departure and Arrival Cards, U.S. Customs Form

Picture 15 — Duty-free Items

Dialogue 1-2-1

Track ∘ 02

Checking cabin facilities and equipment via interphone.

A : Flight Attendant   M : Cabin Manager

A : I'm here in the mid-galley and the temperature of the oven is not rising above 80°C.

M : The mid-galley. Copy[1]. I'll ask the engineer in charge of the cabin to take a look at it. Please let me know once it's been fixed.

---

1) Copy : A response indicating satisfactory receipt of what has just been said on a walkie-talkie or radio.

Substitution Drill 1-2-1

Direction : Practice the conversation with your partner using the information given in the table below.

A : I'm here in (1) _____ and (2) _____ .

M : (1) _____ . Copy. I'll ask the engineer in charge

of the cabin to take a look at it. Please let me know once it's been fixed.

	(1) Location	(2) Problem
A	the upper deck	the coffee maker here isn't working
B	the main deck galley	the elevator is out of order
C	the first class galley	the refrigerator is operating too hot

Dialogue 1-2-2   Track ∘03

Checking the lavatory facilities via interphone.

A : Flight Attendant   M : Cabin Manager

A : The color of the temperature indicator of the lavatory in front of the L2
    door[2] has changed. Please replace it.

M : Copy. Any other problems?

A : No, nothing else.

_____
2) L2 door : The second door on the left

Substitution Drill 1-2-2

Direction : Practice the conversation with your partner using the information given in the table below.

A : (1) _____ . Please (2) _____ .

M : Copy. Any other problems?

A : No, nothing else.

	(1) Problem	(2) Suggested solution
A	There isn't much liquid left in the fire extinguisher	ask the engineer to have it filled with more liquid
B	The toilet isn't flushing properly	check with the engineer in charge of the cabin
C	The water gauge indicates that there is insufficient water	make sure that water is filled up

Dialogue 1-2-3   Track 04

Checking the CIQ forms.

> M : Cabin Manager   A : Flight Attendant

M : Please check the number of U.S.A. arrival forms for the boarding passengers.

A : I've checked the number of customs declaration forms and confirmed we have the three required types of immigration forms, I-94, I-94T, and I-94W.

M : How about the CIQ forms for the return to Korea. Have you checked them too?

A : Yes, there are enough forms for customs, immigration, and quarantine.

Substitution Drill 1-2-3

Direction : Practice the conversation with your partner using the information given in the table below.

M : Please check the (1) _____.

A : I've checked the number of (2) _____.

M : How about the CIQ forms for the return to (3) _____.

　　Have you checked them too?

A : Yes, there are enough forms for customs, immigration, and quarantine.

	(1) Forms	(2) Specific forms to check	(3) Point of departure
A	landing forms for Korea	CIQ forms	U.S.A.
B	CIQ forms	necessary forms	Dubai
C	arrival forms	quarantine and immigration forms	Tokyo

Dialogue 1-2-4   Track ⌒05

Checking duty-free items.

> C : Catering Personnel   A : Flight Attendant
>
> M : Cabin Manager

C : Would you please check the seal number of the duty-free item cart?

A : Yes. I've just done that. I'm signing here.

C : Yes, thank you. Could you please also check the number of items and let me know if it's correct?

A : According to the inventory on the POS[3] system, we are missing two Lancôme compacts. Please look into this.

M : Okay. ... (after a while) ... I've arranged for them to be delivered. Please make sure they're loaded.

---

3) POS stands for point-of-sale indicating the point at which a customer pays a salesperson in exchange for goods or services.

Substitution Drill 1-2-4

Direction : Practice the conversation with your partner using the information given in the table below.

C : Would you please check the seal number of the duty-free item cart?

A : Yes. I've just done that. I'm signing here.

C : Yes, thank you. Could you please also check (1) _____ and let me know if it's correct?

A : According to the inventory on the POS system we are missing (2) _____. Please look into this.

M : Okay. ... (after a while) ... I've arranged for them to be delivered. Please make sure they're loaded.

	(1) The quantity/kinds of items	(2) The insufficient items
A	the quantity of the products	2 Sulwhasoo essences
B	the kinds of items	1 BVLGARI eau de toilette for men
C	the quantity of items	1 Ballentine's 30 Year Old bottle of whisky

3) Checking Special Service Requests (특별 서비스 요청 사항 점검하기)

 Objective Duties (학습 목표)

1. 객실 서비스 규정에 따라 승객 탑승 전, 해당 항공기의 특별 서비스 항목을 점검하고 조치할 수 있다.

2. 객실 서비스 규정에 따라 승객 탑승 전, 해당 승객의 특별 서비스 용품이 탑재되어 있는지를 점검하고 조치할 수 있다.

3. 고객 서비스 규정에 따라 승객 탑승 후, 해당 승객의 특별 서비스 요청 사항 외 추가 요청사항이 없는지를 확인하고 조치할 수 있다.

Words and Phrases (어휘와 어구)

1. special service request^(SSR) 특별 서비스 요청

2. special service item 특별 서비스 용품

3. wheelchair^(WCHR) 휠체어

4. unaccompanied minor^(UM) 미성년자

5. properly 적절히, 제대로

6. stretcher 들것

7. installed 설치된, 설비된

8. portable 휴대용

9. oxygen tank 산소탱크

10. as per ~에 따라

11. pregnant 임신한

12. extension 길게 하는 것, 연장하는 것

13. braille book 점자 책

14. get off 비행기 등에서 내리다

Dialogue 1-3   Track 06

Checking special passengers and their special service items.

M : Cabin Manager   A : Flight Attendant

M : Today's passenger list indicates that there is one passenger who uses a wheelchair (WCHR) and one unaccompanied minor (UM). Have you checked whether a wheelchair and a child's meal have been loaded?

A : Yes. I've confirmed that the wheelchair is loaded and works properly. I've also checked that a child's meal (CHML) has been loaded for the unaccompanied minor (UM).

Substitution Drill 1-3

Direction : Practice the conversation with your partner using the information given in the table below.

M : Today's passenger list indicates that there is (1) _____.

Have you checked whether (2) _____ ?

A : Yes. I've confirmed that (3) _____.

(4) _____.

	(1) Special passenger	(2) Special services/ requests/ items to check	(3) Confirming special services/requests/ items	(4) Additional services/ requests/items
A	1 passenger on a stretcher	the appropriate medical equipment has been loaded	the medical stretcher has been correctly installed	I've also checked that two other additional portable oxygen tanks have been loaded as per the request
B	1 pregnant passenger	there are any additional requests	there are no additional requests	I've also confirmed that seat belt extensions are loaded for the pregnant passenger
C	1 blind passenger	some braille books have been loaded	the braille books have been loaded	I've checked that he can get off the plane first

Additional Information

Abbreviations for Classes, Zones, and Titles.

F/C : First Class

B/C = **C/C**(used by Korean Air) : Business Class

E/Y (Economy Class) = **Y/C** (Economy Class) = **T/C** (Travel Class)

BL : Zone B left side of E/Y

BR : Zone B right side of E/Y

CL : Zone C left side of E/Y

CR : Zone C right side of E/Y

FS : First Class Senior Attendant

FG : First Class Galley Attendant

FJ : First Class Junior Attendant

BS : Business Class Senior, B/C Senior

BG : Business Class Galley, B/C Galley

BJ : Business Class Junior, B/C Junior

TS : Travel Class (E/Y) Senior

Passenger Boarding and Pre-departure Service - Part 1
승객탑승 및 이륙 전 서비스

1) Standing at the Boarding Station (탑승 위치 대기하기)

 Objective Duties (학습 목표)

1. 객실 서비스 규정에 따라 승객의 항공기 탑승 전 각자에게 부여된 임무를 수행하기 위하여 해당 근무지역에서 탑승을 위해 대기할 수 있다.

2. 객실 서비스 규정에 따라 승객 탑승 시 대기 자세를 취할 수 있다.

3. 객실 서비스 규정에 따라 승객 탑승 시 밝은 표정으로 환영 인사를 할 수 있다.

4. 객실 서비스 규정에 따라 탑승 승객에 따른 눈높이 서비스 자세를 취할 수 있다.

Words and Phrases (어휘와 어구)

1. boarding station 탑승 지점

2. assigned 할당된

3. service area 근무 지역, 서비스 지역

4. boarding process 탑승 절차

5. on board 탑승한, 승선한

6. seat number 좌석 번호

7. aisle 복도

8. row 열, 줄

Picture 1 — Inside the Cabin

Dialogu 2-1   Track ○07

Standing and greeting passengers at the assigned service area.

M : Cabin Manager   A : Flight Attendant   P : Passenger

M : We're ready to start the boarding process. Please stand at your assigned service area. (This will be spoken over the interphone.)

A : Okay.

(After a while, while passengers are boarding)

M : How are you? We're pleased to have you on board. This is flight KE202 to Los Angeles.

A : It's nice to have you on board.

P : Hi! Where is seat number 22A?

M : Take the aisle on the right. It is the window seat in the second row.

P : Thank you.

Substitution Drill 2-1

Direction : Practice the conversation with your partner using the information given in the table below.

M : We're ready to start the boarding process. Please stand at your assigned

service area.(This will be spoken over the interphone.)

A : Okay.

(After a while, while passengers are boarding)

M : How are you? We're pleased to have you on board. This is (1) _____ .

A : It's nice to have you on board.

P : Hi! Where is seat number (2) _____ ?

M : Take the aisle (3) _____ . It is (4) _____ .

P : Thank you.

	(1) Flight number	(2) Seat number	(3) Direction	(4) Location of the seat
A	OZ822 to Paris	55D	to the left	the aisle seat in the 5th row
B	AA156 to Dallas	62A	on your right	the window seat in the last row
C	SQ601 to Singapore	31E	on the left	the seat next to the aisle seat in the third row

2) Reconfirming the Boarding Pass (탑승권 재확인하기)

 Objective Duties (학습 목표)

1. 객실 서비스 규정에 따라 승객의 출발 일시를 확인할 수 있다.

2. 객실 서비스 규정에 따라 승객의 목적지를 파악할 수 있다.

3. 객실 서비스 규정에 따라 승객의 좌석 등급을 구별할 수 있다.

4. 객실 서비스 규정에 따라 승객의 좌석번호를 확인할 수 있다.

Picture 2 — A Boarding Pass

Words and Phrases (어휘와 어구)

1. boarding pass   탑승권, 보딩패스

2. welcome aboard   탑승을 환영합니다

3. bother   귀찮게 하다, 성가시게 하다

4. reconfirm   재확인 하다

5. aviation law   항공법

Picture 3 — Boarding Passes

Dialogue 2-2

Track 08

Confirming boarding passes at the boarding station(aircraft door).

A : Flight Attendant   P : Passenger

A : Good afternoon sir/ma'am. Welcome aboard. This is flight KL518 to Amsterdam. May I see your boarding pass?

P : It was checked a moment ago at the airport gate. Why do you want to check it again?

A : I'm sorry to bother you, but we have to reconfirm the boarding pass according to aviation law.

P : Okay. Here it is.

A : Your seat is 35J, which is a window seat. Please take the aisle to the left.

Substitution Drill 2-2

Direction: Practice the conversation with your partner using the information given in the table below.

A : Good afternoon, sir/ma'am. Welcome aboard. This is flight (1) _____ .

　　May I see your boarding pass?

P : It was checked a moment ago at the airport gate. Why do you want to

　　check it again?

A : I'm sorry to bother you, but we have to reconfirm the boarding pass

　　according to aviation law.

P : Okay. Here it is.

A : Your seat is (2) _____ , which is (3) _____ . Please

　　take the aisle to the left.

	(1) Flight number	(2) Seat number	(3) Location of the seat
A	AF762 to Paris	J in the row 22	right next to the window.
B	BA233 to London	31H	an aisle seat.
C	LH401 to Berlin	G in the next row	an aisle seat in the row 45.

3) Showing Passengers to Their Seats (좌석 안내하기)

 Objective Duties (학습 목표)

1. 객실 서비스 규정에 따라 승객들에게 지정된 좌석번호를 재확인할 수
   있다.

2. 객실 서비스 규정에 따라 좌석 배열을 파악하고 승객에게 정확한 좌석
   으로 안내할 수 있다.

3. 객실 서비스 규정에 따라 승객에게 좌석 설비 사용법을 안내할 수 있다.

4. 객실 서비스 규정에 따라 좌석 상태를 파악하여 조치할 수 있다.

Words and Phrases (어휘와 어구)

1. show A to B   A에게 B를 보여주다, 안내하다

2. double seat   한 좌석에 두 명의 승객이 배정된 상황

3. go wrong   실수하다, 잘못하다

4. ground staff   지상 직원

5. inconvenience   불편, 애로

6. got it   알았습니다

7. guide A to B   A를 B로 안내하다

8. separate seats   두 명의 동승 객이 떨어진 좌석에 배정된 상황

9. get married   결혼하다

10. we've just got married   방금 결혼했습니다

11. on one's honeymoon   신혼여행 중이다

12. seating arrangement   좌석 배열

13. at the back   후방에/뒤 쪽에

14. do you mind ~ing?   ~해도 괜찮으시겠습니까?

15. appreciate   고마워하다/인정하다

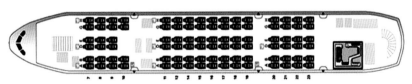

Picture 4 — Aircraft Seat Arrangement - A380 Upper Deck

Dialogue 2-3-1

Track 09

Double seat : Helping in a situation when two passengers are assigned to the same seat.

P1 : Passenger 1   P2 : Passenger 2   A : Flight Attendant

P1 : Excuse me, miss. This is my seat but somebody else is sitting in it.

A : May I see both of your boarding passes, please? Both of you are assigned to seat 15A. Let me check with the ground staff and then I'll explain what went wrong and how I can help you.

(after a while)

A : Thank you for waiting. I'm sorry for the inconvenience. I'm going to show both of you to your seats. (to Passenger 2) Your seat number is 15A. (to Passenger 1) And your seat is 17A. Right over there.

P1 : Okay. Got it.

A : I'm sorry for the inconvenience.

Substitution Drill 2-3-1

Direction : Practice the conversation with your partner using the information given in the table below.

P1 : Excuse me, miss. This is my seat but somebody else is sitting in it.

A : May I see both of your boarding passes, please? Both of you are assigned to seat (1) _____. Let me check with the ground staff and then I'll (2) _____.

(after a while)

A : Thank you for waiting. I'm sorry for the inconvenience. I'm going to show both of you to your seats. (to Passenger 2) Your seat number is (1) _____. (to Passenger 1) And your seat is (3) _____. Right over there.

P1 : Okay. Got it.

A : I'm sorry for the inconvenience.

	(1) Double seat number	(2) What to do after check	(3) Seat for Passenger 1
A	35C	tell you what happened	45C
B	18E	let you know your seat number	22F
C	51D	guide you to your seat	47B

Dialogue 2-3-2   Track 10

Separate seat - Part 1 : Helping in a situation when two passengers travelling together have been assigned separate seats.

P : Passenger   A : Flight Attendant

P : Excuse me, we've just got married and we're on our honeymoon, but we've been assigned separate seats. We'd like to sit next to each other.

A : I'm really sorry about that. I'm going to check the seating assignment and I'll see what I can do so you can sit next to each other. May I see your boarding passes first?

(after a while)

A : Thank you for waiting. I've confirmed that there are two empty seats at the back. Do you mind moving?

P : Not at all. Thank you very much.

Substitution Drill 2-3-2

Direction : Practice the conversation with your partner using the information given in the table below.

P : Excuse me, we are (1) _____, but we've been assigned

separate seats. We'd like to sit next to each other.

A : I'm really sorry about that. I'm going to check the seating assignment

and I'll see what I can do so you can sit (2) _____.

May I see your boarding passes first?

(after a while)

A : Thank you for waiting. I've confirmed that there are two empty seats

(3) _____. Do you mind moving?

P : Not at all. Thank you very much.

	(1) Social distance	(2) Location	(3) New location
A	friends	close to each other	in the front
B	sisters	next to each other	in the middle
C	husband and wife	as close as possible to each other	in the 5th row

Dialogue 2-3-3   Track 11

Separate seat - Part 2 : Helping in a situation when two passengers travelling together have been assigned separate seats.

P1 : Passenger 1   P2 : Passenger 2   A : Flight Attendant

P1 : I'm travelling with my child, but we've been assigned separate seats. Could we sit next to each other?

A : I'm very sorry for the inconvenience. I'll check the seating arrangement. Please let me see your boarding passes first.

....

A : (to another passenger sitting next to an empty seat) Excuse me, sir/ma'am. A passenger and her child in the front have been assigned separate seats. Would it be possible for you to move to a seat in the front so that they can travel together?

P2 : Certainly. What is the seat number?

A : Thank you. You can move to 12B. Let me help you.

(after a while)

A : A passenger sitting next to an empty seat has agreed to change seats so that you and your child can sit next to each other.

P1 : That's very kind of her. I/We really appreciate it. Please say thank you to him/her for us.

Substitution Drill 2-3-3

Direction : Practice the conversation with your partner using the information given in the table below.

P1 : I'm travelling with my (1) _____, but we've been assigned separate seats. Could we sit next to each other?

A : I'm very sorry for the inconvenience. I'll check the seating arrangement. Please let me see your boarding passes first.

....

A : (to another passenger sitting next to an empty seat) Excuse me, sir/ma'am. A passenger and her (1) _____ have been assigned separate seats. Would it be possible for you to move to a seat (2) _____ so that they can travel together?

P2 : Certainly. What is the seat number?

A : Thank you. You can move to (3) _____. Let me help you.

(after a while)

A : A passenger sitting next to an empty seat has agreed to change seats so that you and your (1) _____ can sit next to each other.

P1 : That's very kind of her. I/We really appreciate it. Please say thank you to him/her for us.

	(1) Relation	(2) Location	(3) Seat number
A	little daughter	at the back	62C
B	little son	in another row	35B
C	grandmother	next to the emergency door	42A

Passenger Boarding and Pre-departure Service - Part 2
승객탑승 및 이륙 전 서비스

1) Securing Baggage (수화물 정리 지원하기)

 Objective Duties (학습 목표)

1. 객실 서비스 규정에 따라 좌석 주변의 공간을 파악하여 승객에게 객실 선반의 위치를 안내할 수 있다.

2. 객실 서비스 규정에 따라 안전하게 선반을 작동할 수 있다.

3. 객실 서비스 규정에 따라 수하물의 특성별로 보관하도록 안내할 수 있다.

4. 객실 서비스 규정에 따라 수하물을 안전하게 다룰 수 있다.

5. 객실 서비스 규정에 따라 수하물의 보관 위치를 기억하여, 승객에게 다시 전달할 수 있다.

1. secure 확보하다, 가방 등을 안전하게 두다

2. stow 집어 넣다, 짐을 싣다

3. locate ~에 두다, 위치를 찾다

4. overhead bins 선반

5. compartment 칸, 객실

6. usable 사용 가능한

7. inconvenient 불편한

8. pull down 내리다, 잡아 내리다

9. lift 들어 올리다

10. click 찰칵(딸깍)하는 소리를 내다

11. dimension 공간의 크기 치수

12. stored 보관된

13. fall out 떨어져 나가다

14. place 두다, 놓다

15. drop out 떨어지다

16. coatroom 코트룸

17. package 꾸러미

18. mess up 엉망으로 만들다

19. musical instrument 악기

20. lean 기대다

21. interfere with ~를 방해하다

22. emergency 비상

23. evacuation 탈출

24. contrabass 콘트라베이스

25. timpani 팀파니

26. double-check 재확인하다

27. put away 치우다

28. saxophone 색소폰

Picture 1 — Overhead Bins

Picture 2 — A Flight Attendant Stowing a Passenger's Baggage in an Overhead Bin

Dialogue 3-1-1　　　　　　　　　　　　　Track 12

Locating a usable overhead compartment and explaining its operation.

P : Passenger　　　　A : Flight Attendant

P : Excuse me, miss. My seat is 42A. The bin over my seat is full. Where can I put my baggage?

A : The bin above seat number 42D is empty. If it is not too inconvenient for you, how about using the bin over here?

P : Okay. How can I open this bin?

A : You have to pull down the handle like this. When you want to close it, make sure to lift it up until it clicks.

P : Thank you.

Substitution Drill 3-1-1

Direction : Practice the conversation with your partner using the information given in the table below.

P : Excuse me, miss. My seat is (1) _____. The bin over my seat is full. Where can I put (2) _____?

A : The bin above seat number (3) _____ is empty. If it is not too inconvenient for you, how about using the bin over here?

P : Okay. How can I open this bin?

A : You have to pull down the handle like this. When you want to close it, make sure to lift it up until it clicks.

P : Thank you.

	(1) My seat number	(2) Luggage	(3) Location of an alternative bin
A	62C	my purse	59C
B	35D	this backpack	32A
C	47E	this plastic bag	51D

Dialogue 3-1-2   Track 13

Safely storing baggage according to its dimensions - Part 1.

P : Passenger   A : Flight Attendant

P : May I put this bowling ball in the overhead bin?

A : Heavy items like your bowling ball can be dangerous if stored in the overhead bins. It might fall out during the flight. Would you please place it under the seat in front of you?

P : Sure.

Substitution Drill 3-1-2

Direction : Practice the conversation with your partner using the information given in the table below.

P : May I put this (1) _____. in the overhead bin?

A : Heavy items like your (1) _____ can be dangerous if stored in the overhead bins. (2) _____. Would you please place it (3) _____?

P : Sure.

	(1) Item	(2) Possible danger	(3) Alternative place
A	box	It might drop out of the overhead bin	in the coatroom
B	package	It might fall out during the flight	under the seat in front of you
C	package of kimchi	It might fall out during the flight and mess up the cabin	at the back of the cabin

Dialogue 3-1-3 Track 14

Safely storing baggage according to its dimensions - Part 2.

P : Passenger   A : Flight Attendant

P : The passenger over there has brought a cello onto the plane. Is such a large musical instrument really allowed to be brought onto a plane?

A : Yes. For large and expensive musical instruments such as a cello, passengers may choose to pay for an extra seat. In which case, it's okay for him to lean it on the seat.

P : Okay so why on the window seat?

A : That's because the instrument must not interfere with passengers in an emergency evacuation. Therefore it may only be carried in a window seat, not near the aisle.

P : Okay. I see.

Substitution Drill 3-1-3

Direction : Practice the conversation with your partner using the information given in the table below.

P : The passenger over there has brought a (1) _____ on to the plane. Is such a (2) _____ musical instrument really allowed to be brought onto a plane?

A : Yes. For (3) _____ musical instruments such as a (1) _____, passengers may choose to pay for an extra seat. In which case, it's okay for him to lean it on the seat.

P : Okay so why on the window seat?

A : That's because the instrument must not interfere with passengers in an emergency evacuation. Therefore it may only be carried in a window seat, not near the aisle.

P : Okay. I see.

	(1) Musical instrument	(2) Description	(3) Further description
A	a contrabass	bulky and heavy	large and heavy
B	a timpani	heavy	heavy and bulky
C	a gayaguem	long	long and heavy

Dialogue 3-1-4

Track 15

Returning stored baggage.

A : Flight Attendant   P : Passenger

A : This suitcase is too heavy to store in the overhead compartment and it's too large to store under the seat in front of you. If you don't mind, I'll place it in the coatroom.

P : Sure. When will I be able to get it back?

A : When the plane arrives at the destination, I'll return it to you. May I double-check your seat number? (Attach a tag to the baggage and put it away.)

(after arrival)

A : Thank you for waiting. Here is your suitcase we stored in the coatroom for you.

P : Thank you very much.

Substitution Drill 3-1-4

Direction : Practice the conversation with your partner using the information given in the table below.

A : This (1) _____ is too heavy to store in the overhead compartment and it's too large to store under the seat in front of you. If you don't mind, I'll place it in the coatroom.

P : Sure. When will I be able to get it back?

A : (2) _____, I'll return it to you. May I double-check your seat number? (Attach a tag to the baggage and put it away.)

(after arrival)

A : (3) _____. Here is your (1) _____ we stored in the coatroom for you.

P : Thank you very much.

	(1) Luggage	(2) Time to return luggage	(3) Expressing appreciation
A	box	As soon as we land	I appreciate your cooperation.
B	musical instrument case	When we arrive	Thank you for waiting
C	saxophone	Once we arrive	We appreciate your understanding and cooperation

2) Supporting Special Service Passengers (특수 고객 지원하기)

 Objective Duties (학습 목표)

1. 객실 서비스 규정에 따라 특수 고객 탑승 여부를 확인할 수 있다.

2. 객실 서비스 규정에 따라 특수 고객의 특성에 따른 인사를 하고 좌석을 안내할 수 있다.

3. 객실 서비스 규정에 따라 특수 고객에게 기내 설비 사용법을 안내할 수 있다.

4. 객실 서비스 규정에 따라 특수 고객에 대한 여행 편의를 제공할 수 있다.

Picture 3 — Providing UMs with Some Information

Picture 4 — Giving Service to an Unaccompanied Minor

Words and Phrases (어휘와 어구)

1. special service request form^(SSR form) 특별 서비스 요청서

2. National Assembly 국회

3. minister 장관

4. Foreign Affairs 외교부

5. elderly 노인

6. medical patient 환자

7. comfort 편안, 안락

8. operate 조작하다, 작동하다

9. lever 레버, 지렛대

10. unfold 펼치다

11. guide dog 안내견

12. cabin safety book 기내 안전에 관한 안내서

13. foot rest 발판

14. armrest 팔걸이

15. recline 기울이다

16. entertainment system control 오락물 제공 시스템 조작기

17. omelet 오믈렛

18. oriental noodles 동양식 국수

19. lasagna 라자냐(이타리아 요리)

Dialogue 3-2-1   Track 16

Checking the boarding of special service passengers.

M : Cabin Manager   A : Flight Attendant

M : (Looking at an SSR form) We have Mr. J. K. Kim, a member of the National Assembly in seat number 2A and an unaccompanied minor in seat number 10C. Please make sure that they are on board.

A : Sure. Both Mr. J. K. Kim, in seat number 2A and the UM in seat number 10C have completed boarding.

Picture 5 — Training Cabin Crew How to Guide Blind Passengers

Substitution Drill 3-2-1

Direction : Practice the conversation with your partner using the information given in the table below.

M : (Looking at an SSR form) We have (1) _____ in seat number

(2) _____ and (3) _____ in seat number (4) _____.

Please make sure that they are on board.

A : Sure. Both (1) _____ in seat number

(2) _____ and the (3) _____ in seat number

(4) _____ have completed boarding.

	(1) Special passenger 1	(2) Seat number	(3) Special passenger 2	(4) Seat number
A	Mrs. J. S. Lee, Minister of Foreign Affairs	3A	blind man	15B
B	Mr. and Mrs. K. Y. Park, the President of Bank of Korea and his wife	1A and 1B	elderly lady in a wheel chair	32D
C	Mr. Y. S. Choi, the Chairman of Taeyang Group	1C	medical patient	23C

Dialogue 3-2-2   Track 17

Providing a blind person with information on his/her seat, cabin facilities and equipment, and other travelling comforts.

A : Flight Attendant   P : Passenger

A : How are you sir/ma'am? I'm your flight attendant, Mina Lee.

P : Hello, how are you? Thank you for your help.

A : I'll show you to your seat and explain how to operate your seat. There is a table right in front of you. May I hold your hand to show you how to turn this lever to unfold the table (holding his/her hand softly)? It makes a little noise when it opens. I'm sure you have already been informed about your guide dog. He/She should remain sitting under your seat, and we'll provide him/her with water during the flight.

P : Yes, I was told this before boarding.

A : A cabin safety book and some reading materials written in braille have been prepared for you. Let me know when you'd like them. Have a nice trip.

Substitution Drill 3-2-2

Direction : Practice the conversation with your partner using the information given in the table below.

A : How are you sir/ma'am? I'm your flight attendant, (1) _____.

P : Hello, how are you? Thank you for your help.

A : I'll show you to your seat and explain how to operate your seat.

(2) _____. May I hold your hand to show you how to

(3) _____ (holding his/her hand softly)? (4) _____.

I'm sure you have already been informed about your guide dog. He/She

should remain sitting under your seat, and we'll provide him/her with

water during the flight.

P : Yes, I was told this before boarding.

A : A cabin safety book and some reading materials written in braille have

been prepared for you. Let me know when you'd like them. Have a nice

trip.

	(1) Your name	(2) Explanation 1	(3) Explanation 2	(4) Explanation 3
A	Your name	The button for the foot rest is here.	push the button	You can place your feet here.
B	Your name	There is a button inside your armrest to recline your seat	push the button to recline your seat	Don't be surprised when the seat reclines
C	Your name	There is an entertainment system control inside the armrest	find which button is for music and which one is for the radio	You can use this button to adjust the volume

Dialogue 3-2-3　　　　　　　　　　　　　　　Track ○18

Providing an UM with information on his/her seat, cabin facilities and equipment, and other travelling comforts.

A : Flight Attendant　　　　UM : Unaccompanied Minor

A : Hello, there. I'm your guide, Mina Lee, a cabin crew member of this flight. What's your name?

UM : Hi! My name is Hansol Lee.

A : Your seat is 20A right over here.

UM : I'm a little nervous because I'm travelling alone.

A : Don't worry. I'll put your baggage in the overhead bin. Let me take out some things you may need from your bag before putting it away.

UM : Please give me my color pencils and my notebook.

A : Sure, here they are. Do you like to draw pictures? We have a little gift for you. I'll give it to you before take-off. You can draw pictures with it.

UM : Thank you very much. Can I play games here?

A : You can play games and watch movies on the screen in front of you by using the entertainment system control attached to the armrest. Let me help you with your seatbelt. The total flying time to LA is 9 hours and 30 minutes. Your meal will be provided 30 minutes after departure. I'll serve you your meals as requested by your mother. The first meal is spaghetti and the second one is an omelet. If you want to go to the lavatory or need any of my help, please push this button. Have a nice trip.

Substitution Drill 3-2-3

Direction : Practice the conversation with your partner using the information given in the table below.

A : Hello, there. I'm your guide, (1) _____, a cabin crew member of this flight. What's your name?

UM : Hi! My name is (2) _____.

A : Your seat is 20A right over here.

UM : I'm a little nervous because I'm travelling alone.

A : Don't worry. I'll put your baggage in the overhead bin. Let me take out some things you may need from your bag before putting it away.

UM : Please give me my color pencils and my notebook.

A : Sure, here they are. Do you like to draw pictures? We have a little gift for you. I'll give it to you before take-off. You can draw pictures with it.

UM : Thank you very much. Can I play games here?

A : You can play games and watch movies on the screen in front of you by using the entertainment system control attached to the armrest. Let me help you with your seatbelt. The total flying time to LA is 9 hours and 30 minutes. Your meal will be provided (3) _____ after departure. I'll serve you your meals as requested by your mother. The first meal is (4) _____ and the second one is (5) _____. If you want to go to the lavatory or need any of my help, please push this button. Have a nice trip.

	(1) Your name	(2) Child's name	(3) When to serve meal	(4) First meal	(5) Second meal
A	your name	So-yeon Park	soon	a hamburger	oriental noodles
B	your name	Jung-im Ko	1 hour	pizza	gimbap
C	your name	Jiwoo Kim	40 minutes	fried chicken	lasagna

3) Welcome Aboard In-flight Announcement (탑승 환영 안내 방송하기)

 Objective Duties (학습 목표)

1. 객실 서비스 규정에 따라 방송에 필요한 정보를 파악할 수 있다.

2. 객실 서비스 규정에 따라 탑승 환영 안내 방송에 필요한 언어를 구사할 수 있다.

3. 객실 서비스 규정에 따라 탑승 환영 안내 방송에 필요한 표준어 사용을 할 수 있다.

Words and Phrases (어휘와 어구)

1. entire crew 전 승무원

2. bound for ~행의

3. upright 똑바른, 수직의

4. electronic device 전기기구

5. prohibited 금지된

6. attribute A to B A를 B의 덕분(탓)으로 여기다

7. delayed 지연의

8. dense fog 짙은 안개

9. congestion 혼잡

10. immigration control area 출입국 관리 구역

11. transit station 환승역

12. crew change 승무원 교체

13. unscheduled 미리 계획되지 않은

14. stopover 단기 체류

15. deviation 탈선, 일탈

16. original flight plan 원래 비행 계획

17. seasonal headwind 계절적 맞바람

18. ensure 보장하다, 반드시 ~하게 하다

19. on behalf of ~를 대신(대표)하여

20. launch 시작하다, 착수하다

21. re-operate 재 가동하다

22. extend one's deepest appreciation 깊은 감사를 전하다

23. inaugural 첫, 개회의

Example Announcement 1

Excerpted from : Asiana Airlines In-flight Announcement Passages.

1. WELCOME :

Good morning/afternoon/evening, ladies and gentlemen. Captain _____ and the entire crew would like to welcome you aboard _____ Airlines flight _____ bound for _____. Our flight time will be _____ hour(s) _____ minutes. Please make sure your seat belt is securely fastened, and please return your seat and tray table to their upright position. We'd like to kindly remind you that the use of electronic devices including mobile phones is not allowed during take-off and landing. Smoking in the cabin and lavatories is prohibited at all times during the flight. We're pleased to have you on board today and we look forward to ensuring you have a pleasant flight with us. Thank you.

Example Announcement 2

Excerpted from : Korean Air In-flight Announcement Passages.

2-1. WELCOME AT ORIGINAL STATION[4] : GENERAL

■ Including Joint Operation[5]

Good morning/afternoon/evening, ladies and gentlemen. Captain (FAMILY NAME) and the entire crew would like to welcome you aboard Korean Air, a member of SKYTEAM, flight _____ bound for (via   ).

[JOINT OPERATION]	
Welcome aboard Korean Air, a member of SKYTEAM flight _____, (AIRLINE) flight _____ bound for _____ (via _____). This flight is operated by Korean Air and (AIRLINE).	
DELAY (10 MINUTES OVER)	Reason attributed to the airline: We are sorry for the delay.
	Reason not attributed to the airline: Today we are delayed due to ※ _____.

Our flight time to _____ will be _____ hour(s) _____ minutes.

---

4) Original station : Airport of departure
5) Joint operation : Codeshare flight

> **[R/S JOINING]**[6]
>
> On this flight, we have (a) (NAME OF CITY, NAME OF COUNTRY) - based cabin crew on board.

If there is anything we can do to make your flight more comfortable, our cabin crew is happy to serve you. We hope you enjoy the flight. Thank you.

※ **Delays caused not by the airline company**

1. Bad weather
2. Other weather conditions
3. Dense fog at _____ airport
4. Snow being removed from the runway
5. Congestion at the immigration control area

2-2. WELCOME AT TRANSIT STATION : WHEN THERE ARE JOINING PAX[7]

Ladies and gentlemen, we are now ready to continue our flight to

_____.

> **[GENERAL]**
>
> And we would like to welcome those passengers who joined us in

---

6) R/S Joining: Introducing an overseas crew member whose nationality is that of the destination
7) PAX : Passengers

[CREW CHANGE]

We would like to let you know that there has been a crew change and we would also like to welcome those passengers who joined us in _____ .

[GENERAL]

This is Korean Air, a member of SKYTEAM, Flight _____ bound for _____ (via _____).

[JOINT OPERATION]

This is Korean Air, a member of SKYTEAM, Flight _____ (AIRLINE)

Flight _____ bound for _____ (via _____). This flight is a joint service operated by Korean Air and (AIRLINE).

DELAY (10 MIN-UTES OVER)	Reason attributed to the airline : We are sorry for the delay.
	Reason not attributed to the airline: Today we are delayed due to ※ _____ .

Our flight time to _____ will be _____ hour(s) _____ minutes. If there is anything we can do to make your flight more comfortable, our cabin crew will be happy to serve you. We hope you enjoy the flight. Thank you.

※ **Delays caused not by the airline company**

1. Bad weather
2. Other weather conditions
3. Dense fog at _____ airport
4. Snow being removed from the runway
5. Congestion at the immigration control area

2-3. WELCOME AT TRANSIT STATION : WHEN THERE IS NO JOINING PAX OR AT TECHNICAL LANDING STATION[8]

Welcome back aboard, ladies and gentlemen. We are ready to continue our flight to _____ .

[CREW CHANGE]

There has been a crew change here in _____ .

Our flight time to _____ will be _____ hour(s) _____ minutes. Our cabin crew is looking forward to ensuring you have a pleasant flight. We hope you enjoy the flight. Thank you.

2-4. WELCOME AT TRANSIT STATION : ANNOUNCING AN UNSCHEDULED STOPOVER

■ **When there is a deviation from the original flight plan**

Good morning/afternoon/evening, ladies and gentlemen.

[DIRECT]

Welcome aboard Korean Air non-stop service to _____ .

[STOP OVER]

Welcome aboard Korean Air flight _____ bound for _____ via _____ .

Due to seasonal headwinds, we will have a short stopover at _____ airport.

---

8) Technical landing station : Alternative landing airport in an emergency, which is pre-designated

Our flight time to _____ will be _____ hour(s) _____ minutes. Our cabin crew is looking forward to ensuring you have a pleasant flight. We hope you enjoy the flight. Thank you.

2-5. WELCOME SPECIAL : SEASONAL GREETINGS

■ Welcome at original station announcement

2-5-1. GREETINGS ON THE FIRST DAY OF A NEW YEAR

Happy New Year, ladies and gentlemen. On behalf of Captain (FAMILY NAME) and the entire crew, welcome aboard Korean Air, a member of SKYTEAM, flight _____ bound for _____.
Our flight time to _____ will be _____ hour(s) _____ minutes. Our cabin crew is looking forward to ensuring you have a pleasant flight. We hope you enjoy the flight. Thank you.

2-5-2. GREETINGS ON THE LUNAR NEW YEAR'S DAY

Good morning/afternoon/evening, ladies and gentlemen. On behalf of Captain (FAMILY NAME) and the entire crew, welcome aboard Korean Air, a member of SKYTEAM, flight _____ bound for _____.
It is our great pleasure to have you on board/ for the Lunar New Year. Our flight time to _____ will be _____ hour(s) _____.
Our cabin crew is looking forward to ensuring you have a pleasant flight. Thank you.

2-5-3 CHOOSUK : KOREAN THANKSGIVING DAY

Good morning/afternoon/evening, ladies and gentlemen. On behalf of Captain (FAMILY NAME) and the entire crew, welcome aboard Korean Air, a member of SKYTEAM, flight _____ bound for _____.
It is our great pleasure to have you on board for Choosuk, which is Korean Thanksgiving Day. Our flight time to _____ will be _____ hour(s) _____ minutes after take-off. Our cabin crew is looking forward to ensuring you have a pleasant flight. We hope you enjoy the flight. Thank you.

2-5-4 CHRISTMAS EVE AND CHRISTMAS DAY

Merry Christmas, ladies and gentlemen. On behalf of Captain (FAMILY NAME) and the entire crew, welcome aboard Korean Air, a member of SKYTEAM, flight _____ bound for _____. It is a pleasure to have you with us. Our flight time to _____ will be _____ hour(s) _____ minutes. Our cabin crew is looking forward to ensuring you have a pleasant flight. We hope you enjoy the flight. Thank you.

2-6. SPECIAL WELCOME :

2-6-1 WELCOME SPECIAL : LAUNCHING A NEW ROUTE

■ **When a new route has been launched**

■ **When re-operating an airline**

Good morning/afternoon/evening, ladies and gentlemen. On behalf of Captain (FAMILY NAME) and the entire crew, welcome aboard Korean Air, a member of SKYTEAM, flight _____ bound for _____ (via _____). We would like to extend our deepest appreciation to all passengers on board this (inaugural) flight. Our flight time to will be _____ hour(s) _____ minutes. Our cabin crew is looking forward to ensuring you have a pleasant flight. Thank you.

2-6-2 ANNOUNCEMENT ON A GIVEAWAY SVC[9] FOR THE INAU-GURAL FLIGHT

Ladies and gentlemen, Korean Air is offering a special giveaway for this (inaugural) flight between _____ and _____ . We hope you have a pleasant trip. Thank you.

---

9) SVC : Service

Additional Information 1

An Excerpt from Korean Air Homepage on Service Information for UM and Pregnant Passengers

Excerpted from : www.koreanair.com 2015.07.15

1. Unaccompanied Minors

At Korean Air, we want to provide you with peace of mind when it comes to your children travelling alone on both domestic and international flights. Our staff will accompany them from their departure point through to their destination, making sure the journey is safe and comfortable every step of the way.

If you have any questions or want more specific details about our services, please do not hesitate to contact our Service Center. We understand how stressful this experience can be and want to do all we can to gain your complete trust in Korean Air.

Domestic Flights

• Unaccompanied minors (UM) between the ages of 5 and 12 are eligible for this complimentary service.
• You will need to purchase a standard child fare.

International Flights

• Unaccompanied minors between the ages of 5 and 11 are eligible for this service.
• For any international flight, you will need to purchase a standard adult fare.
• If your children are adolescents between the ages of 12 and 16, they are eligible for Unaccompanied Minor Service on any of our international flights (ID Discount Fares and Special Fares are excluded). There is, however USD 100 service fee required for each child each way (CAD 100, if departing from Canada).

• If your children are travelling to or from Canada, the Philippines or Vietnam, please make note of the special requirements below.

UM Service to Canada
UM Service to the Philippines
UM Service to Vietnam

To apply, please contact Korean Air at least 24 hours prior to your child's departure. You will need to provide appropriate identity and contact information of the parent/guardian for both departure and arrival destinations.

What to Expect During the Trip

At check-in, your children will be given an Unaccompanied Minors badge, alerting the airport staff of their special status.

From that point on, your children will be escorted through each phase of the flight by our trained and capable staff who follow set guidelines to ensure their safety and your peace of mind.

At the destination airport, a dedicated Koran Air attendant will wait with your children until the designated, previously identified adult guardian arrives.

NOTE : If the designated adult fails to come, children will be returned to the departure city at the expense of the sending guardian.

2. Pregnancy

As part of our commitment to our customers, pregnant women who fly internationally will be treated to a complimentary amenity kit that includes skin care products, teas and more.

Simply inform the booking agent when making your reservation or at least 24 hours in advance of departure.

Pregnancy Timetable for Safe Travel

Single Pregnancy (1 child in utero)

• Less than 32 weeks, no special requirements.

• 32-36 weeks, indicate your term during booking and present your declaration form during check-in.

• 37 weeks or more, air travel is prohibited for safety reasons.

Multiple Pregnancy (2 or more children in utero)

• Less than 32 weeks, no special requirements.

• 32 weeks, indicate your term during booking and present your declaration form during check-in.

• 33 weeks or more, air travel is prohibited for safety reasons.

Required Documents

   If you are experiencing complications (gestational hypertension, gestational diabetes, obstetrical hemorrhage, as examples), you must present the following travel documents at check-in.

Medical Certificate

• 1 copy, issued and signed by an OB/GYN.

• Doctor's Note for Air Travel during Pregnancy

Declaration form

• 1 copy, which you need to fill out and sign.

• Declaration Form

Additional Information 2

Air Passenger's Departure Guide - Prohibited Items List

Excerpted from : www.koreanair.com 2015.07.15

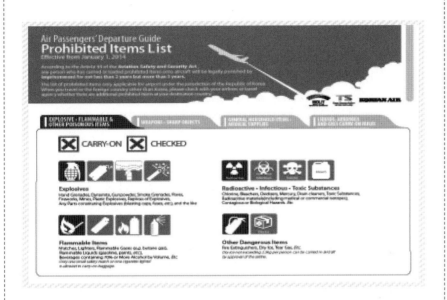

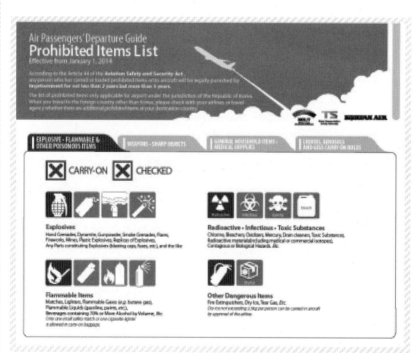

In-flight Service - Part 1
비행 중 서비스 - Part 1

1) Offering Drinks (기내 음료 제공하기)

 Objective Duties (학습 목표)

1. 객실 서비스 규정에 따라 비알콜 음료(Cold Beverage, Hot Beverage)에 관한 정보를 승객에게 전달할 수 있다.

2. 객실 서비스 규정에 따라 다양한 칵테일 제조에 필요한 술의 종류와 첨가 음료에 관한 정보를 숙지하여 제조할 수 있다.

3. 객실 서비스 규정에 따라 다양한 와인에 관한 정보를 파악하여 서비스 및 회수할 수 있다.

 Words and Phrases (어휘와 어구)

1. cocktail tool 칵테일 제조 기구

2. non-alcoholic drink 비알콜 음료

3. call button 호출 단추

4. back 돌아오다

5. green tea 녹차

6. red tea 홍차

7. jasmine tea 재스민 차

8. ginseng tea 인삼차

9. instant 인스턴트(커피)

10. drip coffee 드립식 커피

11. ginger ale 진저에일(생강 맛 탄산음료)

12. on the rocks 온더락(얼음을 탄)

13. neat 스트레이트

14. brandy 브랜디(술의 일종)

15. Cognac 코냑(프랑스 서부 지방에서 생산되는 질 좋은 브랜디)

16. Armagnac 아르마냐크(프랑스산 브랜디의 일종)

17. Scotch 스카치 위스키

18. bourbon 버번 위스키(옥수수와 호밀로 만든 미국산 위스키)

19. effect 효과

20. intoxicated 취한, 도취한

21. consume 소비하다

22. Bloody Mary 블러디 메리(보드카와 토마토 주스를 섞은 칵테일)

23. liquor 독한 술, 독주, 알코올

24. mixer 기주에 첨가하는 비알콜 음료

25. ingredient 재료, 성분

26. manhattan 맨하탄(칵테일의 일종)

27. gin fizz 진피즈(진에 탄산수, 레몬 등을 탄 칵테일)

28. orange blossom 오렌지 블러섬(칵테일의 일종)

29. wine cooler 와인 쿨러(포도주에 과일 주스, 얼음, 소다수를 넣어 만든 칵테일)

30. spritzer 스프리처(백포도주에 소다수를 혼합한 음료)

31. Buck's Fizz 벅스 피즈(샴페인과 오렌지 주스를 섞은 칵테일)

32. vodka 보드카

33. tonic 탄산음료

34. screwdriver 스크류드라이버(칵테일의 일종)

35. gin 진

36. Tom Collins 톰 콜린스(진에 레몬즙, 소다수, 얼음을 넣은 칵테일)

37. red snapper 레드 스냅퍼(진, 토마토 주스, 레몬 주스 등을 넣은 칵테일)

38. gin buck 진벅(칵테일 종류)

39. dry martini 드라이 마티니(쌉쌀한 베르무트에 진을 넣어 만드는 칵테일)

40. dessert wine 디저트 와인(식후 와인)

41. sparkling wine 발포 포도주

42. Shiraz 시라즈(레드와인의 일종)

43. cabernet sauvignon 카베르네 소비뇽(프랑스 보르도 지방에서 재배되는 레드 와인)

44. pinot noir 피노 느와(레드 와인의 일종)

45. merlot 멜로(레드 와인의 일종)

46. Cono Sur 칠레의 코노 수르 지역

47. selection 선택

48. Semillon 세미용(화이트 와인의 일종)

49. Chardonnay 샤르도네(화이트 와인의 일종)

50. Sauvignon Blanc 쇼비뇽 블랑(화이트 와인의 일종)

51. Riesling 리슬링(화이트 와인의 일종)

52. Rhine region 독일의 라인 강 유역

53. sherry 셰리(화이트 와인의 종류)

54. port 포트와인(포르투갈 도루 강 계곡에서 자란 포도 품종으로 만든 포도주 일종)

55. Douro Valley 포르투갈에 위치한 도루 계곡

56. Crémant d'Alsace 크레망 달자스(프랑스 알자스 지역에서 생산되는 탄산 와인의 일종)

57. Champagne 샴페인(탄산 와인의 일종)

58. Blanquette de Limoux 블랑켓 드 리무(탄산 와인의 일종)

59. Moscato d'Asti 모스까또 다스띠(화이트 와인의 일종)

Picture 1 — Cocktail Tools

Picture 2 — Serving Wine in F/C

Dialogue 4-1-1   Track 19

Serving non-alcoholic drinks - Part 1.

> P : Passenger   A : Flight Attendant

P : (Pushing the call button for a flight attendant)

A : Yes, sir/ma'am? How can I help you? Would you like something?

P : Yes, can I have a cup of hot coffee?

A : Sure. How would you like your coffee? Would you like it with milk or sugar?

P : Only sugar, please.

A : Certainly, I'll be back soon with your coffee.

Substitution Drill 4-1-1

Direction : Practice the conversation with your partner using the information given in the table below.

P : (Pushing the call button for a flight attendant)

A : Yes, sir/ma'am? How can I help you? Would you like something?

P : Yes, can I have (1) _____?

A : Sure. How would you like (2) _____? Would you like

it (3) _____?

P : (4) _____, please.

A : Certainly, I'll be back soon with (2) _____.

	(1) Non-alcoholic drink	(2) Non-alcoholic drink	(3) Alternatives	(4) How you would like it
A	a cup of tea	your tea	with milk or lemon	Tea with lemon
B	a can of 7-up	your 7-Up	with some ice	Yes, 7-up with ice
C	a glass of orange juice	your orange juice	with some ice	No, without ice

Dialogue 4-1-2 Track 20

Serving non-alcoholic drinks - Part 2.

A : Flight Attendant   P : Passenger

A : We're serving some drinks before dinner. What can I get you?

P : May I have a cup of tea?

A : We have green tea, red tea, jasmine tea, and ginseng tea. Which one would you like?

P : Can I have red tea?

A : How would you like your red tea, sir/ma'am? We have milk, lemon, and sugar.

P : I'd like to have it with milk.

A : Okay, it'll be ready soon.

Picture 3 — Serving Coffee in the Cabin

Substitution Drill 4-1-2

Direction : Practice the conversation with your partner using the information given in the table below.

A : We're serving some drinks before dinner. What can I get you?

P : May I have (1) _____?

A : We have (2) _____. Which one would you like?

P : Can I have (3) _____?

A : How would you like your (3) _____, sir/ma'am?

    (4) _____.

P : I'd like to have (5) _____.

A : Okay, it'll be ready soon.

	(1) Drink	(2) Type of drink	(3) Choice	(4) Addition	(5) Drink with addition
A	a cup of coffee	fresh Americano, cafe latte, instant, and drip coffee	Americano	We have milk and sugar	an Americano with sugar
B	a glass of soda	Coke, Diet Coke, Sprite, and ginger ale	ginger ale	Ice or no ice?	a ginger ale with some ice
C	a glass of juice	orange juice, tomato juice, and apple juice	apple juice	Ice or no ice?	an apple juice without ice

Dialogue 4-1-3   Track 21

Serving alcoholic drinks - Part 1.

A : Flight Attendant   P : Passenger

A : Excuse me, sir/ma'am. May I get you a drink?

P : May I have a glass of whisky?

A : On the rocks? Or neat?

P : Whisky on the rocks please.

A : Sure. I'll get you a glass of whisky on the rocks.

Substitution Drill 4-1-3

Direction : Practice the conversation with your partner using the information given in the table below.

A : Excuse me, sir/ma'am. May I get you a drink?

P : May I have (1) _____?

A : (2) _____?

P : (3) _____ please.

A : Sure. I'll get you (4) _____.

	(1) Alcoholic drink	(2) Type of drink	(3) Choice	(4) Amount
A	a can of beer	Cass or Budweiser	Cass	a can of Cass
B	a glass of brandy	Cognac or Armagnac	Cognac	a glass of Cognac
C	a glass of whisky	Scotch or bourbon	Bourbon neat	a glass of bourbon

Dialogue 4-1-4

Track 22

Serving alcoholic drinks - Part 2.

P : Passenger   A : Flight Attendant

P : Can I have two cans of beer and a glass of cognac?

A : I'm very sorry sir/ma'am. We have already served you four glasses of whisky and two glasses of wine. Due to differences in air pressure and the cabin environment, alcohol may have a stronger effect than while on the ground and it's easier to become intoxicated. How about a fresh orange juice instead of beer and cognac?

P : Okay.

Picture 4 — A Flight Attendant Making a Cocktail

Substitution Drill 4-1-4

Direction : Practice the conversation with your partner using the information given in the table below.

P : Can I have (1) _____ ?

A : I'm very sorry sir/ma'am. We have already served you (2) _____ .
Due to differences in air pressure and the cabin environment, alcohol may have a stronger effect than while on the ground and it's easier to become intoxicated. How about (3) _____ instead of (4) _____ ?

P : Okay.

	(1) Alcoholic drink	(2) The alcoholic drinks the passenger has consumed	(3) Non-alcoholic drink	(4) Alcoholic drink
A	a glass of whisky	three glasses of Scotch whisky	some cold 7-Up	whisky
B	two glasses of Cognac	three cans of beer and two glasses of whisky	some fresh apple juice	Cognac
C	a can of beer	three cans of beer	a Coke with ice	beer

Dialogue 4-1-5   Track 23

Serving cocktail - Part 1.

P : Passenger   A : Flight Attendant

P : Is it possible for me to have a Bloody Mary?

A : Yes, of course. We can make many kinds of cocktail with the liquors, mixers, and other ingredients we have.

P : Okay. One Bloody Mary, please.

Picture 5 — Serving A Cocktail in the Cabin

Substitution Drill 4-1-5

Direction : Practice the conversation with your partner using the information given in the table below.

P : Is it possible for me to have a/an (1) _____?

A : Yes, of course. We can (2) _____ with the liquors, mixers, and other ingredients we have.

P : Okay. One (1) _____, please.

	(1) Cocktail	(2) Possibility
A	manhattan	mix several kinds of cocktails
B	gin fizz	prepare various kinds of cocktails
C	orange blossom	make many different kinds of cocktails

Dialogue 4-1-6 Track 24

Serving cocktail - Part 2.

P : Passenger   A : Flight Attendant

P : What kind of cocktails can you make with wine?

A : We could make you a wine cooler, spritzer and Buck's Fizz.

P : I'll go with a Buck's Fizz, please.

A : Certainly. I'll be back soon with your drink.

Picture 6 — Serving Wine in the Cabin

Substitution Drill 4-1-6

Direction : Practice the conversation with your partner using the information given in the table below.

P : What kind of cocktails can you make with (1) _____ ?

A : We could make you a (2) _____.

P : I'll go with a (3) _____, please.

A : Certainly. I'll be back soon with your drink.

	(1) Base	(2) Kinds of cocktail using the base liquor	(3) Choice
A	vodka	vodka & tonic, Bloody Mary, or a screwdriver	vodka & tonic
B	gin	gin & tonic, gin fizz, orange blossom, Tom Collins, red snapper, gin buck, dry martini, etc.	gin & tonic
C	bourbon	bourbon & Coke or a manhattan	manhattan

Dialogue 4-1-7　　　　　　　　　　　Track 25

Serving wine.

A : Flight Attendant　　　P : Passenger

A : Would you like some wine with your meal?

P : What kind of wine do you have?

A : We have red wine, white wine, dessert wine, and sparkling wine.

P : I'd like a glass of red wine. Do you have any Shiraz?

A : I'm sorry but we don't have any Shiraz. We only have cabernet sauvignon, pinot noir, and merlot.

P : Then, I'll go with a merlot.

A : Sure. I'll get you a merlot. This wine was produced in Cono Sur in 2006.

P : Thank you very much.

Picture 7 — Showing a Bottle of Wine to a Passenger

Substitution Drill 4-1-7

Direction : Practice the conversation with your partner using the information given in the table below.

A : Would you like some wine with your meal?

P : What kind of wine do you have?

A : We have red wine, white wine, dessert wine, and sparkling wine.

P : I'd like a glass of (1) _____. Do you have any
   (2) _____?

A : I'm sorry but we don't have any (2) _____. We only have
   (3) _____.

P : Then, I'll go with a (4) _____.

A : Sure. I'll get you a (4) _____. This wine was produced in
   (5) _____.

P : Thank you very much.

	(1) Type of wine	(2) Choice	(3) Selection	(4) Choice	(5) When and where produced
A	white wine	Semillon	Chardonnay, Sauvignon Blanc, and Riesling	Riesling	the Rhine region of Germany in 2010
B	dessert wine	sherry	port	port	the Douro Valley, Portugal in 2013
C	sparkling wine	Crémant d'Alsace	Champagne, Blanquette de Limoux, and Moscato d'Asti	Moscato d'Asti	Italy in 2011

Additional Information

A Wine List

Excerpted from : Wine List for economy class of Singapore Airlines.

beverages

wine
Red – Blend of Syrah
and Cabernet Sauvignon
White – Chardonnay
White – Riesling

aperitifs
Campari
Dry Vermouth

spirits
Johnnie Walker Red Label Whisky
Jim Beam Black Label Bourbon
Rémy Martin VSOP Cognac
Beefeater Gin
Smirnoff Red Label Vodka
Bacardi Superior Rum

liqueurs
Grand Marnier Cordon Rouge
Bailey's Original Irish Cream

beer
International Selection
Stout

soft drinks
Coke
Coke Light/Coke Zero
7-UP
Ginger Ale
Soda Water
Bitter Lemon

cocktails
Singapore Sling
*Enjoy this 1915 classic
- a concoction of dry gin,
Dom Benedictine, orange
liqueur, and cherry brandy,
shaken with lime and pineapple
juice, a dash of Angostura
bitters, and Grenadine.*

Alspritzer
Screwdriver
Bloody Mary
Dry Martini

mocktails
Fruit Spritzer
Orange Cooler

fruit juices
Orange
Apple
Pineapple
Tomato

coffee and tea
Coffee
Black Tea
Oolong Tea
Pu-Erh Tea
Sencha Green Tea
Peppermint Tea
(naturally caffeine-free)

In-flight Service - Part 2
비행 중 서비스 - Part 2

1) Offering Meals (기내식 제공하기)

 Objective Duties (학습 목표)

1. 객실 서비스 규정에 따라 기내에서 제공되는 식사를 위한 세팅(Setting) 및 데우기 (Heating) 등을 수행할 수 있다.

2. 특별서비스요청서(SSR: Special Service Request)에 따라 특별식을 확인 후, 서비스 및 회수할 수 있다.

3. 객실 서비스 규정에 따라 승객 선호를 확인하여 테이블 매너에 따른 기내식을 서비스 및 회수할 수 있다.

Words and Phrases (어휘와 어구)

1. set meals 음식을 세팅하다(~에 놓다)

2. heat meals 음식을 데우다

3. entrée 주 요리, 앙뜨레

4. occupied 점령한, 차지한

5. headsets 헤드폰, 이어폰

6. served 제공되는

7. keep up the good work 열심히 잘하다

8. landing documents 도착 서류

9. galley attendant 주방을 맡고 있는 승무원

10. rack 선반

11. broth 국물, 스프

12. boil over 끓어 넘치다

13. make a mess 뒤 범벅을 만들다

14. fillet mignon 살코기 스테이크

15. pasta 파스타(이태리식 요리)

16. pork cutlet 포크커틀릿(돈가스)

17. sirloin steak 서로인 스테이크

18. shrimp 새우

19. plastic bag 비닐 봉지

20. utensils 기구, 도구

Picture 1 — E/Y Dinner

21. besides 그 밖에

22. omelet 오믈렛

23. congee 죽

24. scrambled eggs 스크램블드에그(휘저어 부친 계란 프라이)

25. French toast 프렌치토스트(우유와 달걀을 섞어 푼 것에 식빵을 적셔 프라이팬에 구운 빵)

26. cereal 시리얼(곡식을 갈아서 만든 아침 식사)

27. English muffin 영국식 머핀

28. hash browns 해시브라운(감자요리의 일종)

29. minute steak 얇게 저민 스테이크

30. apricot 살구

31. beef stew 비프 스튜(소고기 스튜)

32. combination 조합, 결합

33. enhance 높이다, 향상시키다

34. flavor 맛, 풍미

35. whereas 반면에

36. complement to ~에 대한 보완물

37. Château Moulin de Cassy 품종을 섞어서 만든 혼합 화인의 일종

38. Medoc 프랑스 서남부의 메독 지방

39. blended 혼합한, 섞은

40. full body 감칠맛이 나는

41. tannin 타닌 성분

42. marinated beef 양념된 소고기

43. soy sauce 간장

44. garlic 마늘

45. sesame oil 참기름

46. roasted 구운

47. chicken curry 닭고기 카레요리

48. grilled beef ribs 석쇠에 구운 소 갈비

49. beef stroganoff 소고기 스트로가노프(양파, 버섯, 싸워크림이 들어간 소고기 요리의 일종)

50. green onions 파

51. chestnuts 밤

52. jujubes 대추

Picture 2 — Special Meal Low Fat Meal

Dialogue 5-1-1

Track 26

Setting and heating meals.

> SA : Senior Flight Attendant
>
> A : Flight Attendant in charge of the galley

SA : Please make sure that today's main entrées, beef steak and chicken, are heated before serving.

A : Sure.

SA : Today, all seats are occupied, so we have many passengers to take care of. Make sure that the meals are set to be heated as soon as the plane takes off so that we can serve meals right after headsets and drinks have been offered.

A : Okay, got it. I'll also make sure that the wine to be served with dinner is open on the ground.

SA : Thanks. Keep up the good work.

(in the galley after departure)

SA : Please provide the passengers with landing documents and headsets. The galley attendant and I will place the meals in the cart.

A : I'll take the rack with the main entrées out of oven. Will you please place 24 beef meals and 24 chicken meals in each cart?

SA : The entrées are very hot. Please be careful when you put them in the cart so that broth doesn't boil over and make a mess over the other meals.

A : Okay, got it.

Substitution Drill 5-1-1

Direction : Practice the conversation with your partner using the information given in the table below.

SA : Please make sure that today's main entrées, (1) _____ ,

are heated before serving.

A : Sure.

SA : Today, all seats are occupied, so we have many passengers to take care

of. Make sure that the meals are set to be heated as soon as the plane

takes off so that we can serve meals right after headsets and drinks have

been offered.

A : Okay, got it. I'll also make sure that the wine to be served with dinner is

open on the ground.

SA : Thanks. Keep up the good work.

(in the galley after departure)

SA : Please provide the passengers with landing documents and headsets.

The galley attendant and I will place the meals in the cart.

A : I'll take the rack with the main entrées out of oven. Will you please

place (2) _____ in each cart?

SA : The entrées are very hot. Please be careful when you set them in the cart

so that broth doesn't boil over and make a mess over the other meals.

A : Okay, got it.

	(1) Main entrées	(2) Number of entrées
A	fillet mignon and pasta	30 fillet mignons and 30 pastas
B	pork cutlet and sirloin steak	25 pork cutlets and 25 sirloin steaks
C	chicken and shrimp	24 chickens and 24 shrimps

Dialogue 5-1-2   Track ∘ 27

Checking the SSR form and serving special in-flight meals.

A : Flight Attendant   P : Passenger

A : Are you Mr. Trevor Marshall in seat number 24A?

P : Yes, that's right.

A : The vegetarian meal you requested is ready.

P : Thank you very much.

A : When the meal service starts after takeoff, I'll bring it to you. If there's anything else you need, please let me know.

P : I don't think I'll need anything else. The vegetarian meal will be enough.

Picture 3 — In-flight Breakfast

Substitution Drill 5-1-2

Direction : Practice the conversation with your partner using the information given in the table below.

A : Are you (1) _____ in seat number (2) _____?

P : Yes, that's right.

A : The (3) _____ you requested is ready.

P : Thank you very much.

A : When the meal service starts after takeoff, I'll bring it to you. If there's anything else you need, please let me know.

P : (4) _____.

	(1) Name	(2) Seat number	(3) Special meal	(4) Other requests
A	Ms. Susan King	37C	diabetic meal	Could I please also have a blanket?
B	Mr. Shigero Danaka	45B	low salt meal	I'd like to have a glass of water too, please.
C	Ms. Deepika Kumar	29D	Hindu meal	May I also have a glass of orange juice?

Dialogue 5-1-3   Track 28

Serving a kosher meal.

> A : Flight Attendant   P : Passenger

A : Good morning/afternoon/evening. Are you Ms. Olivia Geller in 34G who requested a kosher meal?

P : Yes, that's me.

A : Your first and second meals are both kosher meals. I need to heat them before serving. Would you please open the meal for heating?

P : (opening one of the boxes) OK. I'll open the plastic bags of bread and utensils once you've served the meal. Please bring me the main entrée when it's heated.

A : Sure. Would you like something to drink besides the one that comes with the meal?

P : The drink in the box is enough for me. Thank you.

  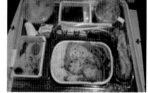

Picture 4 — Kosher Meal

Substitution Drill 5-1-3

Direction : Practice the conversation with your partner using the information given in the table below.

A : Good morning/afternoon/evening. Are you (1) _____ who requested a kosher meal?

P : Yes, that's me.

A : Your first and second meals are both kosher meals. I need to heat them before serving. Would you please open the meal box for heating?

P : (opening one of the boxes) OK. I'll open the plastic bags of bread and utensils once you've served the meal. Please bring me the main entrée when it's heated.

A : Sure. Would you like something to drink besides the one that comes with the meal?

P : (2) _____.

	(1) Passenger's name and seat number	(2) Other drink
A	Mr. Daniel Kaufman in 55E	Can I have some orange juice as well?
B	Mrs. Rachel Cohen in 38C	I'd like to have a Coke too, please.
C	Ms. Yasmin Rosenberg in 27B	I would also like some more water, please.

Dialogue 5-1-4 Track 29

Serving breakfast.

A : Flight Attendant   P : Passenger

A : Excuse me, sir/ma'am, we're serving breakfast now. Today's breakfast is an omelet or congee.

P : I'll have an omelet for me and congee for my child.

A : Would you like some orange juice or coffee?

P : Coffee for me. And for him, orange juice please.

A : Certainly. Enjoy your meal.

Picture 5 — Wine and a Wine Basket

Substitution Drill 5-1-4

Direction : Practice the conversation with your partner using the information given in the table below.

A : Excuse me, sir/ma'am, we're serving breakfast now. Today's breakfast is

(1) _____.

P : I'll have (2) _____.

A : Would you like some (3) _____?

P : (4) _____ please.

A : Certainly. Enjoy your meal.

	(1) Breakfast menu	(2) Choice	(3) Drinks	(4) Choice
A	scrambled eggs and French toast	French toast	apple juice or milk	apple juice
B	cereal & fruit and English muffins	an English muffin	milk or apple juice	milk
C	hash browns and minute steak	a hash brown	Tomato juice or apricot juice	apricot juice

Dialogue 5-1-5

Track 30

Serving dinner.

A : Flight Attendant   P : Passenger

A : Today, we have bibimbap with vegetables and beef stew cooked with red wine for dinner.

P : What is the beef stew?

A : It is a combination of beef and vegetables cooked in a broth. Today's beef stew is cooked with red wine to enhance the flavor.

P : The beef stew sounds nice. I'd like to try it.

A : Okay, I'll get you the red wine beef stew. Would you like to have something to drink with the meal?

P : Which drink would go well with the beef stew?

A : Red wine usually goes better with beef dishes, whereas white wine is a better complement to white meats such as chicken and fish.

P : Okay, I'll have some red wine, please.

A : The red wine I'm going to serve today is a Château Moulin de Cassy produced in Medoc in 2010. It is a blended wine of 50% of Cabernet Sauvignon and 50% of Merlot. Since it is blended, it has full body and tannins. It should go well with today's beef stew.

P : I'm looking forward to the dinner. Thank you very much for your kind explanation.

A : My pleasure. Enjoy your meal.

Substitution Drill 5-1-5

Direction : Practice the conversation with your partner using the information given in the table below.

A : Today, we have (1) _____ and (2) _____ for dinner.

P : What is the (2) _____ ?

A : (3) _____ .

P : The (2) _____ sounds nice. I'd like to try it.

A : Okay, I'll get you a (2) _____ . Would you like something to drink with the meal?

P : Which drink would go well with the (2) _____ ?

A : Red wine usually goes better with beef dishes, whereas white wine is a better complement to white meats such as chicken and fish.

P : Okay, I'll have some red wine, please.

A : The red wine I'm going to serve today is a Château Moulin de Cassy produced in Medoc in 2010. It is a blended wine of 50% of Cabernet Sauvignon and 50% of Merlot. Since it is blended, it has full body and tannins. It should go well with today's (2) _____ .

P : I'm looking forward to the dinner. Thank you very much for your kind explanation.

A : My pleasure. Enjoy your meal.

	(1) Entrée 1	(2) Entrée 2	(3) Explanation of an Entrée
A	beef steak	bulgogi	It is marinated beef with soy sauce, garlic, and sesame oil, and roasted in a pan
B	chicken curry	bulgalbi	It is a dish of marinated and grilled beef ribs
C	beef stroganoff	galbijjim	It is boiled beef ribs marinated with soy sauce, green onions, garlic, sesame oil along with some chestnuts and jujubes

In-flight Service - Part 3
비행 중 서비스 - Part 3

1) Offering In-flight Entertainment Service (기내 오락물 제공하기)

 Objective Duties (학습 목표)

1. 객실 서비스 규정에 따라 기내에서 제공되는 오락물 상영을 위한 기내 시설물과 기물을 사용할 수 있다.

2. 객실 서비스 규정에 따라 비행 중 서비스 되는 상영물에 관한 종류와 내용을 고객에게 전달할 수 있다.

3. 객실 서비스 규정에 따라 조명 및 객실 상태를 점검하고, 오락물을 제공할 수 있다.

Words and Phrases (어휘와 어구)

1. in-flight entertainment service 기내 오락물 서비스

2. Video-On-Demand system VOD 시스템

3. detailed 상세한

4. in-flight magazine 기내 잡지

5. refer 참조하다

6. seat pocket 좌석 주머니

7. operate 작동/가동하다

8. insert 삽입하다

9. headset 수신기

10. jack 잭

11. plug 전기 플러그

12. armrest 팔걸이

13. remove 제거하다

14. remote control 리모컨, 원격조정(기)

15. fantasy movies 판타지영화

16. documentaries 기록물, 다큐멘터리

Picture 1 — In-flight Video System and a Remote Control

Dialogue 6-1   Track 31

Offering in-flight entertainment service.

P : Passenger   A : Flight Attendant

P : Excuse me, miss. What are today's films?

A : We offer a video-on-demand system. You can enjoy a variety of films and entertainment programs on a variety of channels of your choice. For more detailed information, you can refer to the in-flight magazine in the seat pocket in front of you.

P : Oh really! Do you have films for children too?

A : Yes, you can use channel 3 for children's films. You can watch them either in Korean or English by selecting the language you want.

P : Could you tell me how I can operate the system?

A : First of all, you have to insert the headset jack into the outlet in the armrest and remove the remote control which is located inside the armrest. It looks a little like a telephone. You can either push the buttons on the remote control or touch the screen.

P : Thanks.

A : Whenever you need assistance, you can push this button with the picture of an attendant on it.

P : Thank you for your kind explanation.

Substitution Drill 6-1

Direction : Practice the conversation with your partner using the
information given in the table below.

P : Excuse me, miss. What are today's films?

A : We offer a video-on-demand system. You can enjoy a variety of films
and entertainment programs on a variety of channels of your choice. For
more detailed information, you can refer to the in-flight magazine in the
seat pocket in front of you.

P : Oh really! Do you have (1) _____ too?

A : Yes, you can use (2) _____. You can watch
them (3) _____ by selecting the language you want.

P : Could you tell me how I can operate the system?

A : First of all, you have to insert the headset jack into the outlet in the
armrest and remove the remote control which is located inside the
armrest. It looks a little like a telephone. You can either push the buttons
on the remote control or touch the screen.

P : Thanks.

A : Whenever you need assistance, you can push this button with the picture
of an attendant on it.

P : Thank you for your kind explanation.

	(1) Kind of video	(2) Channel	(3) Languages
A	fantasy movies	channel 5 for fantasies	either in English or Chinese
B	TV series	channel 1 for TV series	in English, Korean, or French
C	documentaries	channel 2 for documentaries	in Korean, Japanese, or English

2) Duty-free Items Service (면세품 판매하기)

 Objective Duties (학습 목표)

1. 객실 서비스 규정에 따라 면세품 판매를 위한 기본적인 상품을 세팅하고 판매할 수 있다.

2. 객실 서비스 규정에 따라 국가별 면세품 구매 한도에 관한 정보를 전달할 수 있다.

3. 객실 서비스 규정에 따라 면세품 판매 전, 후 재고파악 및 인수인계를 위한 서류를 정리할 수 있다.

Picture 2 — Displaying Duty-free Items

Words and Phrases (어휘와 어구)

1. get it done ~을 끝내다

2. order form 주문서

3. purchase limit 면세한도액

4. perfume 향수

5. a carton of 한 상자, 한 보루

6. tax 세금, 관세

7. Bobby Brown 바비브라운 화장품(회사)

8. Estée Lauder 에스티 로더 화장품(회사)

9. Clos du val 끌로 뒤 발 미국산 포두주

10. compact 화장 도구, 콤팩트

11. payment method 지불 방법

12. Marlboro 말보로 담배

13. company 동행자

14. Chivas Regal 시버스 리갈

15. keep records 기록하다

16. hand over 넘겨주다, 이양하다

17. seal 봉(인)하다

18. make a final call 마지막으로 부르다

19. last minute shopping 마지막 순간 쇼핑

20. make a final announcement 마지막 안내방송을 하다

Dialogue 6-2-1 　　　　　　　　　Track 31

Selling duty-free items.

A : Flight Attendant　　　P : Passenger

A : Would you like to order any duty-free items?

P : Yes please. I would like to order one Bobby Brown compact, one Estée Lauder eye cream, and two bottles of Clos du val.

A : Are you going to pay in Korean won? Or in US dollars?

P : I want to pay by credit card. Could you please give me the price in US dollars?

A : Fine. I'll get it done for you right away. Would you please write down your seat number and name on the order form?

P : Sure. (.. after completing the form ..) Here it is.

A : For those entering Korea, the purchase limits are a 1-liter bottle of liquor valued at no more than US$400, 2-oz perfume, and one carton of cigarettes. In total, your duty-free purchases may not have a combined value of more than US$600. If you purchase over this limit, you'll have to pay tax on the items. You've bought one Bobby Brown compact, one Estée Lauder eye cream, and two bottles of Clos du val.

P : Yes, I know. My companion and I are buying one bottle of wine each. There'll be no problem with the purchase limits.

A : Okay. I'll bring them to you right away.

Substitution Drill 6-2-1

Direction : Practice the conversation with your partner using the information given in the table below.

A : Would you like to order any duty-free items?

P : Yes please. I would like to order (1) _____ .

A : Are you going to pay in Korean won? Or in US dollars?

P : I want to pay (2) _____ .

A : Fine. I'll get it done for you right away. Would you please write down your seat number and name on the order form?

P : Sure. (.. after completing the form ..) Here it is.

A : For those entering Korea, the purchase limits are a 1-liter bottle of liquor valued at no more than US$400, 2-oz perfume, and one carton of cigarettes. In total, your duty-free purchases may not have a combined value of more than US$600. If you purchase over this limit, you'll have to pay tax on the items. (3) _____ .

P : Yes, I know. (4) _____ . There'll be no problem with the purchase limits.

A : Okay. I'll bring them to you right away.

	(1) Duty-free items	(2) Payment method	(3) Purchase over the limit	(4) Company
A	two cartons of Marlboro and one Sulwhasoo night cream	in Korean won	You've bought two cartons of cigarettes	My brother and I are buying one carton of Marlboro each
B	two bottles of Chivas Regal	in US dollars	You've purchased two bottles of whisky	I'm traveling with my husband.
C	two bottles of Chanel No. 5	in Chinese yuan	You've bought two bottles of perfume	My friend and I are buying one each

Dialogue 6-2-2 Track 33

Checking inventory of duty-free items and keeping records to hand over.

> AD : Flight Attendant in charge of duty-free items.
>
> A : Flight Attendant

AD : It's 30 minutes before landing so I'm going to stop selling duty-free items.

A : Okay.

AD : I'm going to check the inventory and fill out the form to hand over to the next cabin crew team. I'm sealing the duty-free item cart soon. When you make the landing announcement, please make a final call for duty-free sales so that the passengers can do any last minute shopping.

A : Okay. Is there anything else I can help you with?

AD : No, nothing else. Thanks.

Substitution Drill 6-2-2

Direction : Practice the conversation with your partner using the information given in the table below.

AD : (1) _____ so I'm going to stop selling duty-free items.

A : Okay.

AD : I'm going to check the inventory and fill out the form to hand over to the next cabin crew team. I'm sealing the duty-free item cart soon. (2) _____ .

A : Okay. Is there anything else I can help you with?

AD : No, nothing else. Thanks.

	(1) Time before landing	(2) Asking another flight attendant for a favor
A	We'll soon be arriving	Would you please make a final announcement for duty-free sales?
B	We'll be landing in 40 minutes	Please make an announcement that we're closing the duty-free sales soon
C	We'll be reaching our destination in half an hour	Could you do me a favor? Could you make the announcement that the duty-free sales will soon be closed?

3) Checking the Cabin (객실 상태 점검하기)

 Objective Duties (학습 목표)

1. 객실 서비스 규정에 따라 고객 서비스를 위해 객실 시설물을 수시로 점검하고 조치를 할 수 있다.

2. 객실 서비스 규정에 따라 기내식 서비스 후 객실 통로 및 주변을 청결히 할 수 있다.

3. 객실 서비스 규정에 따라 승객의 쾌적한 여행을 위해 객실 내 온도 및 조명을 관리할 수 있다.

Picture 3 ― A Control System for the Cabin Temperature and
Lights Usually Located Above the Jump Seat of Cabin Manager in
the Front of the Cabin

Words and Phrases (어휘와 어구)

1. lights 조명

2. take a rest 쉬다

3. dim 어둡게 하다, 둔화시키다

4. from time to time 가끔, 이따금

5. walk-around service 서비스 장소 안을 이리저리 걷다, 순회 서비스

6. asleep 잠이 든, 자고 있는

7. run out 다 떨어지다

8. amenity 생활 편의시설, 편의용품

Dialogue 6-3-1   Track 34

Checking the cabin.

M : Cabin Manager   A : Flight Attendant

M : Please check the temperature and lights in each service zone and let me
    know if they're at the correct level.

A : Stephanie, the lights in zone D are too bright. Now, all the services are
    done and the passengers are either watching movies or taking a rest.
    Please dim the lights or turn them off.

M : Some passengers are using the lavatory now that they've finished eating.
    I'm dimming the lights and will turn them off in 10 minutes.

A : Okay. One passenger said it was cold. However, others said it was okay.
    I'll just give a blanket to the passenger who said it was cold. I'm going
    to check the temperature from time to time and make sure it remains
    constant.

M : Okay. Now, it's time for the passengers to rest. Please make sure that
    you don't make a lot of noise when you prepare for the next service in
    the galley.

Substitution Drill 6-3-1

Direction : Practice the conversation with your partner using the information given in the table below.

M : Please check the temperature and lights in each service zone and let me know if they're at the correct levels.

A : Stephanie, the lights in zone D are too bright. Now, all the services are done and the passengers are either watching movies or taking a rest. Please dim the lights or turn them off.

M : Some passengers are using the lavatory now that they've finished eating. I'm dimming the lights and will turn them off in 10 minutes.

A : Okay. (1) _____ .

(2) _____ . I'm going to check the temperature

from time to time and make sure (3) _____ .

M : Okay. Now, it's time for the passengers to rest. Please make sure that you don't make a lot of noise when you prepare for the next service in the galley.

	(1) Passengers' complaints regarding temperature	(2) What the cabin crew will do	(3) What the cabin crew will do
A	Some passengers are complaining that it's a bit too warm.	I'll lower the temperature	it stays at the proper temperature
B	Two passengers at the back said it was cold	I'll ask some other passengers how they feel	the temperature in the cabin is fine for most of the passengers
C	One passenger in zone C keeps saying it's too cold for her, although other passengers say it's okay	I'm just going to give her a blanket and some warm water	it isn't too cold

Dialogue 6-3-2

Track 35

Walk-around service.

A1 : Flight Attendant 1　　　A2 : Flight Attendant 2

A1 : Since it's a night flight, a lot of passengers are asleep or resting. Would you please do a continuous walk-around service? And would you please make sure that the service items in the lavatory are not running out?

A2 : Okay. I've checked that the aisles are clear. I'm doing a walk-around service with water and orange juice every 10 minutes.

A1 : The lights are now off. When you walk around the cabin, please be careful. And please respond to any passenger calls.

A2 : Okay.

Substitution Drill 6-3-2

Direction : Practice the conversation with your partner using the information given in the table below.

A1 : Since it's a night flight, a lot of passengers are asleep or resting. Would you please do a continuous walk-around service? And would you please make sure (1) _____?

A2 : Okay. I've checked (2) _____. I'm doing a walk-around service with water and orange juice every 10 minutes.

A1 : The lights are now off. When you walk around the cabin, please be careful. And please (3) _____.

A2 : Okay.

	(1) Thing to check	(2) Thing that's been checked	(3) Second thing to check
A	all the amenities in the cabin are in good condition	that the lavatories are clean and in good condition	check that all passengers are comfortable
B	there are enough service items in the lavatories	the lights are dim enough for passengers to rest comfortably	check if any passengers are too cold
C	the video system is working well	all the service areas are clean and clear	check whether there is anybody who needs assistance

Additional Information 1

In-flight Announcement on Selling Duty-free Items

Excerpted from : Korean Air In-flight Announcement Passages

1. IN-FLIGHT SALES

Ladies and gentlemen,

We are now selling duty-free items and you may now make your purchases or place your orders for your return flight.

Passengers transferring from (name of a country) should contact a cabin crew member when purchasing duty free liquor items. For more information, please refer to the 'Sky Shop' magazine in your seat pocket. If you need any assistance, our cabin crew will be happy to help you.

[The flight attendant in charge of selling duty-free items must check the acceptable amount of duty-free items of Germany and Thailand. (For other countries, when it is necessary)]

We would like to remind you that the duty free allowance for (name of a country) is _____ bottle(s) of liquor and _____ carton(s) of cigarettes.

[In case in-flight sale is not allowed on a certain flight/portion]

Also, we would like to let you know that duty free sales will not be available on the next portion of our flight, between _____ and _____. Thank you.

2-1. CLOSING IN-FLIGHT SALES

Ladies and gentlemen, we will soon be finishing our duty-free sales. However, we would like to remind you that you may purchase duty free items at any time during the flight. If you would like to make any purchases, please contact a cabin crew member.

[On a flight leaving Korea] Also, if you would like to pre-order duty free items for your return flight, please contact a cabin crew member who will be happy to help you.]

2-2. CLOSING IN-FLIGHT SALES

[After approaching signal] Ladies and gentlemen, we regret to announce that we have stopped our duty free sales in preparation for landing. Thank you.

Additional Information 2

Lists of Acceptable Amounts of Duty-free Items for the U.S.A, Japan and China

A list of acceptable amounts of duty-free items for the U.S.A.

Excerpted from : U.S. Customs and Board Protection

Item	Allowance
Alcohol	• up to 1 liter ※ Limited to those aged 21 or older, and for the purposes of consuming or giving as a gift
Tobacco	• 200 cigarettes, 100 cigars ※ If they are made in Cuba, you must get a permit before purchase
Perfume	• Up to 150ml

Item	Allowance
Value limits for duty-free goods	• U.S. visitors (non-resident): up to US$100 worth of goods (if you are visiting the U.S. for 72 hours or more) • Transfer passengers: up to US$200 worth of goods • U.S. residents: up to US$200, US$800, US$1,600 worth of goods depending on how long and where you have traveled 1. Frequent travelers: up to US$ 200 worth of goods 2. U.S. residents returning from countries other than the Caribbean countries or U.S. insular possessions: up to US$800 worth of goods. The next US$1,000 worth of the goods will be subject to a flat rate of 3% 3. U.S. residents returning from U.S. U.S. insular possessions (i.e. Samoa, Guam, or U.S. Virgin Islands): up to US$1,600 worth of goods. The next US$1,000 worth of the goods will be subject to a flat rate of 1.5%
Currency limits	• You must declare currencies or checks worth more than US$10,000

https://help.cbp.gov/app/answers/detail/a_id/454/~/duty-free-exemption%2C-gifts

A list of acceptable amounts of duty-free items for Japan

Excerpted from :Japan Customs

Item		Allowance (for an adult)	Remarks
Alcohol		3 bottles	The average bottle size is 760cc
Tobacco products	Cigars	100 cigars	If a visitor brings in more than one kind of tobacco product, the total allowance is 500grams.
	Cigarettes	400 cigarettes	
	Other kinds of tobacco	500 grams	
Perfume		2 ounces	

Item	Allowance (for an adult)	Remarks
Others	200,000yen	The total overseas market value of all articles other than the above items must be under 200,000yen. Any items whose overseas market value is under 10,000yen is free of duty and/or tax and is not included in the calculation of the total overseas market value of all articles. There is no duty-free allowance for articles having a market value of more than 200,000yen each or each set.

http://www.customs.go.jp/english/summary/passenger.htm

A list of acceptable amounts of duty-free items for China

Excerpted from : China Highlights

Item	Allowance
Alcohol	• Up to 1,500ml. of alcoholic drinks(with alcohol content of 12% or above)
Tobacco	• 400 individual cigarettes, 100 individual cigars, or 500 grams of smoking tobacco
Perfume	• Only for the amount to be used personally during the stay in China
Other goods	• Such items as clothes, hats, handicrafts, and other commodities worth less than RBM 1,000 • Non-resident passengers: a total worth of RMB 2,000. Those exceeding the duty-free limit shall be released subject to payment of customs duty.
Items which may be brought in but must be brought out of China	• One video camera, one portable video recorder, one portable word processor

http://www.chinahighlights.com/travelguide/guidebook/customs.htm

Pre-landing Service
착륙 전 서비스

---

1) Distributing Arrival Forms and Helping Passengers Fill in the Forms (입국 서류 배포 및 작성 지원하기)

 Objective Duties (학습 목표)

1. 객실 서비스 규정에 의해 담당구역별 도착지 입국에 필요한 서류를 배포할 수 있다.

2. 객실 서비스 규정에 따라 도착지 국가의 출입국 규정을 숙지하여 승객에게 정확히 안내할 수 있다.

3. 객실 서비스 규정에 따라 도착 전 입국에 필요한 서류의 작성 여부를 점검하고 조치할 수 있다.

4. 객실 서비스 규정에 의해 특수 고객에게 필요한 서류 작성에 협조할 수 있다.

 Words and Phrases (어휘와 어구)

1. hand out 나누어 주다

2. citizen 시민

3. resident 거주자, 영주권자

4. immigrant visa holder 미국 이민비자 소지자

5. ESTA(Electronic System for Travel Authorization) 미국 전자여행허가제로 비자 면제 프로그램

6. I-94W form 미국입국서류의 일종으로 ESTA 비자면제프로그램이용자를 위한 양식

7. elderly lady 여자 노인

8. relative 친척

9. red pepper paste 고추장

10. pickled sesame leaves 깻잎 장아찌

11. anchovy 멸치

12. list 열거하다, 나열하다

13. plant 식물

14. food products 식료품

15. vacuum packed kimchi 진공 포장된 김치

16. dried seaweed 김

17. dorm 기숙사

18. sesame oil 참기름

19. red ginseng 홍삼

20. pickled olive 절인 올리브

Dialogue 7-1-1 Track 36

Distributing arrival forms and helping passengers fill in the forms - Part 1.

A : Flight Attendant   P : Passenger

A : We're handing out US immigration forms. Is the USA your final destination?

P : Yes.

A : Are you a US citizen, a US resident, a US immigrant visa holder, or a Canadian citizen?

P : No, I'm a Korean tourist visiting the USA.

A : Do you have a US entry visa?

P : No. I have an e-Passport and ESTA.

A : Then, you have to fill in an I-94W form as well as a customs form.

P : There are four of us in my family, so please give me four forms.

A : You only need to fill in one customs form per family.

P : Oh, I see. Thank you.

Substitution Drill 7-1-1

Direction : Practice the conversation with your partner using the information given in the table below.

A : We're handing out US immigration forms. Is the USA your final destination?

P : Yes.

A : Are you a US citizen, a US resident, a US immigrant visa holder, or a Canadian citizen?

P : No, I'm a Korean tourist visiting the USA.

A : Do you have a US entry visa?

P : (1) _____.

A : Then, (2) _____ as well as a customs form.

P : There are (3) _____ of us in my family so please give me

(3) _____ forms.

A : You only need to fill in one customs form per family.

P : Oh, I see. Thank you.

	(1) Whether you have a US visa	(2) Type of form you have to use	(3) Number of people in your family
A	Yes, I do	you must use an I-94 form	five
B	No, I don't but I have applied for ESTA	you need this green I-94W form	three
C	Yes, I do have a US visa	here is an I-94 form for you	two

Dialogue 7-1-2   Track 37

Distributing arrival forms and helping passengers fill in the forms - Part 2.

A : Flight Attendant   P : Passenger

A : (To an elderly lady) Excuse me, ma'am, would you like any help filling in the immigration form?

P : What should I write in the blank for the address in the US?

A : Are you going to stay in a hotel or with a relative?

P : I'll be staying in a hotel.

A : Then you can write down the name of the hotel you'll be staying in.

P : What should I do with this blue form?

A : Do you happen to be carrying any kind of food?

P : I have some red pepper paste, pickled sesame leaves, and some anchovies.

A : In that case you have to write down the names of the items on the back of the form. You have to list all of the animal, plant, and food products you're carrying.

P : Thank you very much

Substitution Drill 7-1-2

Direction : Practice the conversation with your partner using the information given in the table below.

A : (To an elderly lady) Excuse me, ma'am, would you like any help filling in the immigration form?

P : What should I write in the blank for the address in the US?

A : Are you going to stay in a hotel or with a relative?

P : (1) _____.

A : Then (2) _____.

P : What should I do with this blue form?

A : Do you happen to be carrying any kind of food?

P : I have some (3) _____.

A : In that case you have to write down the names of the items on the back of the form. You have to list all of the animal, plant, and food products you're carrying.

P : Thank you very much.

	(1) Where you're staying	(2) What to write in the blank	(3) Food you're carrying
A	I'll be staying at my sister's house	you should write down her address	vacuum packed kimchi and dried seaweed
B	I'll be staying in a dorm	you have to write the location of the dorm	sesame oil and Korean red ginseng
C	I'm going to stay in a guesthouse	do you know the address? You have to write it down	vacuum packed cheese and some pickled olives

2) Collecting In-flight Service Items (기내용품 회수하기)

 Objective Duties (학습 목표)

1. 객실 서비스 규정에 의해 서비스한 기내 용품과 회수된 기내 용품의 수량을 파악할 수 있다.

2. 객실 서비스 규정에 의해 회수된 기내 용품의 상태를 확인하여 상태별로 분리할 수 있다.

3. 객실 서비스 규정에 의해 기내 용품 소지 승객에 대해 회수 안내할 수 있다.

Words and Phrases (어휘와 어구)

1. descent 하강, 내려가기

2. cutting in and out 붙었다 끊어졌다

Dialogue 7-2   Track 38

Collecting in-flight service items.

A : Flight Attendant   P : Passenger

A : Excuse me, I'm collecting the headphones you're using.

P : I'm still watching a movie. Can I give them back to you a little later?

A : I'm very sorry but I have to have all the headphones back before we begin our descent. So I really need to take them back now.

P : Okay.

A : Was everything else okay with you?

P : Actually, the right headphone kept cutting in and out.

A : It must have caused you some trouble. I'm sorry to hear that. I'll let the manager/maintenance staff know about it.

Substitution Drill 7-2

Direction : Practice the conversation with your partner using the information given in the table below.

A : Excuse me, I'm collecting (1) _____ .

P : (2) _____ . Can I give it back to you a little later?

A : I'm very sorry but I have to have (3) _____ back before we begin our descent. So I really need to take them back now.

P : Okay.

A : Was everything else okay with you?

P : Actually, (4) _____ .

A : It must have caused you some trouble. I'm sorry to hear that. I'll let the manager/maintenance staff know about it.

	(1) Item to collect	(2) The thing the passenger is still doing	(3) Items to be collected	(4) Problem
A	the can of beer you've drunk	I'm still drinking it	all the cans and bottles	the remote control for the VOD service didn't work well
B	the meal tray	I'm still eating	all the trays	it was too cold
C	the coffee cup	I haven't finished the coffee yet	all the cups and glasses	the lights were too dim

3) Checking the Inventories of In-flight Service Items and Duty-free Items (기내 서비스 용품 및 면세품 재고 확인하기)

 Objective Duties (학습 목표)

1. 객실 서비스 규정에 따라 기내 판매 업무를 종료하고 면세품 재고를 확인할 수 있다.

2. 객실 서비스 규정에 따라 면세품에 대한 상태를 확인하여 필요 조치를 취할 수 있다.

3. 객실 서비스 규정에 따라 서비스 종료 후 서비스 용품 재고를 확인할 수 있다.

4. 객실 서비스 규정에 따라 하기 시 필요한 조치사항과 교대 팀에게 필요한 전달 사항을 기록할 수 있다.

Words and Phrases (어휘와 어구)

1. **coffee pillow** 커피팩, 커피봉지

2. **order sheet** 주문서

3. **consume** 소모하다, 먹다, 마시다

4. **slip** 전표, 표, 가늘고 긴 종이

5. **currency** 통화, 화폐

6. **calculate** 계산하다, 산출하다

7. **Chinese yuan** 중국 위안화

Dialogue 7-3　　　　　　　　　　　　　　　Track 39

Checking the inventories of in-flight service items and duty-free items.

> M : Cabin Manager　　A1 : Flight Attendant 1
>
> A2 : Flight Attendant 2

M : Have you checked the inventory of the in-flight service items?

A1 : Yes, I have. The next flight is fully booked. I've ordered 50 Cokes, 30 7-Ups, 200 plastic cups, and 10 coffee pillows. Here is the order sheet.

M : Have you made out a liquor list too?

A1 : Yes. I've written how much liquor has been consumed and put the slip inside the cart. I've also sealed the cart.

M : What about the duty-free items? Have you checked the inventory of the duty-free items too?

A2 : Yes, it's correct.

M : Today, we've received many different currencies such as dollars, yen, and euros. So please pay special attention when calculating. Please write carefully and correctly about the items that should be loaded for the next team.

A2 : Okay. Got it.

Substitution Drill 7-3

Direction : Practice the conversation with your partner using the information given in the table below.

M : Have you checked the inventory of the in-flight service items?

A1 : Yes, I have. The next flight is fully booked. I've ordered (1) _____ .

Here is the order sheet.

M : Have you made out a liquor list too?

A1 : Yes. I've written how much liquor has been consumed and put the slip inside the cart. I've also sealed the cart.

M : What about the duty-free items? Have you checked the inventory of the duty-free items too?

A2 : Yes, it's correct.

M : Today, we've received (2) _____ . So please pay special attention when calculating. Please write carefully and correctly about the items that should be loaded for the next team.

A2 : Okay. Got it.

	(1) New ordered items	(2) Currencies
A	5 bottles of orange juice, 20 ginger ales, 30 Cokes, and 20 Sprites	won, yuan, and US dollars
B	15 coffee pillows, 20 tea bags, and 3 bottles of tomato juice	US dollars, euros, and Korean won
C	35 plastic cups, 10 paper towels, and 20 bottles of water	Japanese yen, euros, US dollars, Chinese yuan, and Korean won

4) Announcement of the Arrival at the Destination
(목적지 도착 안내 방송 하기)

Objective Duties (학습 목표)

1. 객실 서비스 규정에 따라 방송에 필요한 정보를 파악할 수 있다.

2. 객실 서비스 규정에 따라 목적지 도착 안내방송에 필요한 언어를 구사 할 수 있다.

3. 객실 서비스 규정에 따라 목적지 도착 안내방송에 필요한 표준어 사용을 할 수 있다.

Words and Phrases (어휘와 어구)

1. have ~ ready ~를 준비하다

2. health questionnaire 건강 질문서

3. equivalent 동등한, 맞먹는

4. seeds 씨앗, 종묘

5. pick up ~를 집다, 들어올리다

6. re-boarding 재탑승

7. transit area 갈아 타는 곳

8. make descent 하강하다

9. window shade 블라인드

10. clear customs 세관을 통과하다

11. guidance 지도, 안내

Example Announcement 1

Excerpted from : Korean Air In-flight Announcement Passages.

1. ARRIVAL INFORMATION: KOREA

Ladies and gentlemen,

Please have your entry documents ready for entry into Korea.

All passengers are required to complete an arrival card and customs form

(and a health questionnaire).

Thank you.

Example Announcement 2

Excerpted from : Korean Air In-flight Announcement Passages.

2. ARRIVAL INFORMATION: USA

Ladies and gentlemen,

Please have your entry documents ready for entry into the United States.

Passengers carrying more than ten thousand US dollars, or the equivalent

in foreign currency must declare the amount on the customs form.

Fruits, plants, seeds, or other food items must also be declared.

[T/S FLT]¹⁰⁾

Those passengers continuing on to _____ are also required to take all belongings with them and clear customs here at _____ airport after picking up all your checked baggage. Re-boarding will begin in approximately _____ minutes.

The boarding time will be announced in the transit area.

Thank you.

 Example Announcement 3

Excerpted from : Asiana Airlines In-flight Announcement Passages

3. HEADPHONE COLLECTION

Ladies and gentlemen,

We hope you have enjoyed our entertainment program.

Our flight attendants will collect your headphones shortly.

Your cooperation is much appreciated.

Thank you.

---

10) T/S FLT : transit fligth

Example Announcement 4

Excerpted from : Asiana Airlines In-flight Announcement Passages.

4. 10,000 ft. SIGN ON

Ladies and gentlemen,

We're now making our descent into _____(airport name)_____.

Please return your seat and fasten your seat belt, and return your seat back and tray table to their upright position.

We'd also like to ask you to open the window shade nearest you.

Please make sure your bags are stowed in the overhead bins or under the seat.

All electronic devices such as personal computers, CD players and electronic games should now be turned off.

Thank you.

Example Announcement 5

Excerpted from : Asiana Airlines In-flight Announcement Passages

5. TRANSIT PROCEDURE

Ladies and gentlemen,

For those passengers with a connecting domestic flight, please pick up all checked baggage and clear customs here at Incheon International Airport.

Please transit at the domestic check-in counter either at Incheon International Airport or at Gimpo Airport.

When you pick up your baggage, please check that your baggage tag number and claim tag number match correctly.

Passengers with connecting international flights, please follow the guidance of our ground staff.

Thank you.

 Example Announcement 6

Excerpted from : Asiana Airlines In-flight Announcement Passages

6. LANDING

Ladies and gentlemen,

We're now making our final approach.

Please make sure your seat belt is fastened.

Please also check that your seat back is in the upright position and your tray table is closed.

Thank you.

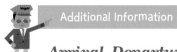

Additional Information

Arrival, Departure, and Customs Forms of China and Arrival and Departure Forms of Japan

1. Arrival and Departure Forms of China

Excerpted from : Asiana Airlines Homepage

http://vishubs.tistory.com/5

2. Customs Forms of China

Excerpted from : China Eastern Homepage

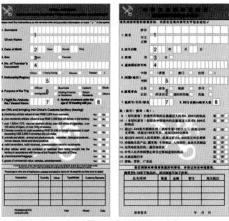

①성명 ②생년월일 ③성별 ④여권번호 ⑤국적 ⑥입국사유 ⑦항공편명 ⑧16세미만 동반소아

http://uilove.egloos.com/m/3022712

3. Arrival and Departure Forms of Japan

Excerpted from : Incheon International Airport

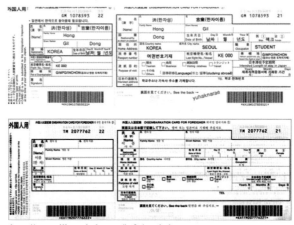

http://www.ilbonuhak.com/info/ready.htm
http://airport.or.kr/airport/inout/depart_02_4_pop2.htm

Unit 08

Post - landing Service
착륙 후 서비스

1) Landing Announcement (도착 안내방송하기)

 Objective Duties (학습 목표)

1. 객실 서비스 규정에 따라 착륙 후 도착 안내방송(Farewell) 실시할 수 있다.

2. 객실 서비스 규정에 따라 여권과 입국서류 소지 안내방송을 실시할 수 있다.

3. 객실 서비스 규정에 의거 해당 공항에 따른 상황별 안내방송을 할 수 있다.

Words and Phrases (어휘와 어구)

1. refrain from ~ing ~하는 것을 자제하다

2. switch on 스위치를 켜다

3. valued 평가된, 가격이 산정된, 값이 매겨진

4. quarantined 검역을 받는

5. unsatisfactory 만족스럽지 못한

6. dense fog 짙은 안개

Example Announcement 1

Excerpted from : Asiana Airlines In-flight Announcement Passages

1. FAREWELL

Ladies and gentlemen,

It's our pleasure to welcome you to Los Angeles International Airport.

The local time (here in _____) is _____ am/pm (on Monday, March 4).

For your safety, please keep your seat belt fastened until the captain turns off the seat belt sign.

Also, refrain from switching on your mobile phone until you are in the airport terminal.

When opening the overhead bins, please be careful of contents that may have moved during the flight.

Before leaving the aircraft, please check that there're no items left in your seat pocket or under your seat.

Please make sure you have all of your carry-on baggage with you when you leave the aircraft.

On behalf of the entire crew, we've enjoyed serving you today and we hope to see you soon.

Thank you.

 Example Announcement 2

Excerpted from : Asiana Airlines In-flight Announcement Passages.

2. DOCUMENTATION: KOREA

Ladies and gentlemen,

Please have your passport and other entry documents ready for entry into Korea.

If you are carrying any items valued over the duty free allowance or more than _____ U.S dollars or the equivalent in foreign currency, you must declare it on the customs form.

If you are carrying any kind of fruit, plant or meat products, they must be declared on the customs form and may need to be quarantined.

Passengers who have baggage arriving on another aircraft or by ship must fill out two customs forms.

For further details, please contact a flight attendant.

Thank you.

2) Helping Passengers Disembark (승객 하기 지원하기)

Objective Duties (학습 목표)

1. 도착지 공항 규정에 따라 검역 또는 세관의 허가가 필요한지 확인할 수 있다.

2. 객실 서비스 규정에 따라 승객 하기 시 감사하는 마음으로 하기 인사를 실시할 수 있다.

3. 객실 서비스 규정에 의해 승객의 짐 운반 등을 적극적으로 도움을 줄 수 있다.

Words and Phrases (어휘와 어구)

1. in line   줄을 서서

2. asleep   잠이 든

3. skip   건너 뛰다, 거르다

4. miss   거르다, 놓치다

Dialogue 8-2   Track ⊙ 40

Helping passengers disembark. (Some flight attendants are standing at the aircraft door and the passengers are getting off in line. The important thing here is to say farewell appropriately according to various types of passengers.)

| A : Flight Attendant | P1 : Passenger 1 |
| P2 : Passenger 2 | P3 : Passenger 3 |

A : Thank you very much. Good-bye.

P1 : Thanks for your help.

A : Your child was asleep during the meal service. I'm afraid she may be hungry.

P2 : She is fine. Thank you for your kindness.

A : Have a nice trip. I hope to see you again on your way home.

P2 : Thanks again.

A : (To a honeymooner) Congratulations on your wedding. Have a wonderful honeymoon.

P3 : Thank you very much.

Substitution Drill 8-2

Direction : Practice the conversation with your partner using the information given in the table below.

A : Thank you very much. Good-bye.

P1 : (1) _____ .

A : (2) _____ .

P2 : (3) _____ . Thank you for your kindness.

A : Have a nice trip. I hope to see you again on your way home.

P2 : Thanks again.

A : (4) _____ .

P3 : Thank you very much.

	(1) Expressing gratitude	(2) Expressing concern for passengers	(3) Explaining things are okay	(4) Wishing the passengers a pleasant stay
A	You did a great job	You skipped your dinner. I hope you aren't hungry	I'm all right	Congratulations on getting a new job in the United States.
B	You were very kind	Your daughter missed lunch. I hope she isn't hungry	She doesn't feel good and doesn't want to eat anything.	Have a wonderful time with your son's family
C	I appreciate your help	I hope you're not too tired from working on your paper.	I'm fine	Have a nice family reunion

3) Assisting Special Service Passengers (특수 고객 지원하기)

 Objective Duties (학습 목표)

1. 객실 서비스 규정에 따라 지상직원에게 여객 및 화물 운송 관련 서류(Ship pouch)를 인계하고 중요 승객이나 특별 승객에 대한 정보를 구두로 먼저 알려줄 수 있다.

2. 객실 서비스 규정에 따라 응급환자, VIP, F/C, C/C, Y/C, UM, Stretcher(환자) 승객 순으로 신속히 하기가 이루어질 수 있도록 안내할 수 있다.

3. 객실 서비스 규정에 따라 특수 고객을 위해 적극적으로 게이트(Gate)까지 지원할 수 있다.

Words and Phrases (어휘와 어구)

1. stroller 유모차

2. cargo 화물

3. disembarkation 하기, 하선, 하륙

4. get mixed up 얽히게 된다

5. in the order of ~의 순서로

6. place 놓다

7. get into it 올라타다, 들어가다

8. purse 여성용 가방

Dialogue 8-3-1 $\qquad$ Track ∘41

Assisting special service passengers.

M : Cabin Manager　　GS : Ground Staff

M : Good morning/afternoon/evening. We have one UM and one passenger in a wheelchair. The passenger in seat number 24B wants to have her baby stroller back.

GS : Okay. The wheelchair and the stroller are coming up from cargo to the aircraft door. Have you told the two passengers that they might have to wait a little bit at the door?

M : Yes, I have. I'll have the passenger in the wheelchair get off last. The passenger with the stroller told me she is going to wait at the door. I'm going to hand over the UM first.

GS : Any problems with the UM?

M : Well, she wasn't able to eat much, but everything else was fine.

GS : Thank you.

Substitution Drill 8-3-1

Direction : Practice the conversation with your partner using the information given in the table below.

M : Good morning/afternoon/evening. We have one UM and one passenger in a wheelchair. (1) _____ wants to have her baby stroller back.

GS : Okay. The wheelchair and the stroller are coming up from cargo to the aircraft door. Have you told the two passengers that they might have to wait (2) _____?

M : Yes, I have. I'll have the passenger in the wheelchair get off last. The passenger with the stroller told me (3) _____. I'm going to hand over the UM first.

GS : Any problems with the UM?

M : Well, she wasn't able to eat much, but everything else was fine.

GS : Thank you.

	(1) Seat number of the passenger with a stroller	(2) Time to wait	(3) What the passenger will do
A	The woman in seat number 53A	for 10 minutes	she will wait for the stroller
B	The passenger in seat number 31D	for a while	she will get off slowly
C	The young lady in seat number 10D	for a few minutes	she will want the stroller delivered as soon as possible

Dialogue 8-3-2 | Track 42

The order of disembarkation on a B747(when both L1 Door and L2 Door are open)

M : Cabin Manager   A1 : Flight Attendant 1
A2 : Flight Attendant 2

M : Today both the L1 door and the L2 door will be open for disembarkation. We've got to pay special attention when our 450 passengers get off. Those flight attendants who are in charge of the L1 door have to be careful so that the B/C passengers of the upper deck and the passengers of the main deck in zone B do not get mixed up.

A1 : Today the passengers will get off in the order of the 5 F/C passengers, the 32 B/C passengers, and then the Y/C passengers in zone B.

M : Then, how are you going to have the rest of the Y/C passengers get off?

A2 : They will get off in the order of zone C, zone D, and zone E. Since there are two aisles, the R (right) side aisle passengers will have to walk through the galley. The zone C attendants have to stand and say good-bye to the R side aisle passengers at the galley.

M : That sounds fine. Since we have a full aircraft today please make sure we maintain a high standard of service until the disembarkation is complete.

Substitution Drill 8-3-2

Direction : Practice the conversation with your partner using the information given in the table below.

M : Today both the L1 door and the L2 door will be open for disembarkation. We've got to pay special attention when our (1) _____ passengers get off. Those flight attendants who are in charge of the L1 door have to be careful so that the B/C passengers of the upper deck and the passengers of the main deck in zone B do not get mixed up.

A1 : Today the passengers will get off in the order of the (2) _____ F/C passengers, the (3) _____ B/C passengers, and then the Y/C passengers in zone B.

M : Then, how are you going to have the rest of the Y/C passengers get off?

A2 : They will get off in the order of zone C, zone D, and zone E. Since there are two aisles, the R (right) side aisle passengers will have to walk through the galley. The zone C attendants have to stand and say good-bye to the R side aisle passengers at the galley.

M : That sounds fine. Since we have a full aircraft today please make sure we maintain a high standard of service until the disembarkation is complete.

	(1) Number of total passengers	(2) Number of F/C passengers	(3) Number of B/C passengers
A	510	7	29
B	495	3	35
C	505	6	26

Dialogue 8-3-3

Track 43

Providing a special service passenger with assistance from his/her seat to the aircraft door (when a passenger has to use a cabin wheelchair from his/her seat and then change to his/her own wheelchair at the door.).

A : Flight Attendant   PW : Passenger in a Wheelchair

A : How was your flight? Was everything okay?

PW : Well, I wasn't used to the wheelchair so I had some difficulties when using the lavatory.

A : I'm sorry about that sir/ma'am. The cabin wheelchair was made small to fit the cabin space.

PW : You helped me a lot so I didn't feel uncomfortable. Thank you very much.

A : Not at all. Your wheelchair is waiting for you at the aircraft door.

PW : Oh really? It'll be good to have my wheelchair as soon as possible.

A : Let me help you. Now, you can change to your wheelchair.

PW : Please place my wheelchair right next to this one. I'll get into it by myself.

A : Okay. I'm holding them both for you.

PW : Whew, that's better.

A : Let me help you place your legs on the foot rests. Your baggage has been handed over to the ground staff.

PW : Thank you so much.

A : My pleasure. I hope to see you again.

Substitution Drill 8-3-3

Direction : Practice the conversation with your partner using the information given in the table below.

A : How was your flight? Was everything okay?

PW : (1) _____ .

A : I'm sorry about that sir/ma'am. The cabin wheelchair was made small to fit the cabin space.

PW : You helped me a lot so I didn't feel uncomfortable. Thank you very much.

A : Not at all. Your wheelchair is waiting for you at the aircraft door.

PW : Oh really? It'll be good to have my wheelchair as soon as possible.

A : Let me help you. Now, you can change to your wheelchair.

PW : Please place my wheelchair right next to this one. I'll get into it by myself.

A : Okay. I'm holding them both for you.

PW : Whew, that's better.

A : Let me help you place your legs on the foot rests. (2) _____ .

PW : Thank you so much.

A : My pleasure. I hope to see you again.

	(1) Discomfort	(2) Baggage
A	The wheelchair was a bit too small for me	Your purse is right here
B	The aisles were too narrow and the wheelchair was too small for me	The ground staff will help you with your bag
C	It was difficult to move around	You only have one small purse.

Cheeking the Cabin after Disembarkation
승객 하기 후 관리

1) Checking for Lost Property (유실물 점검하기)

 Objective Duties (학습 목표)

1. 객실 서비스 규정에 따라 승객 하기 후 유실물 점검을 최우선으로 하며 상위 클래스일 경우 지상조업 개시 전에 철저히 점검을 실시할 수 있다.
2. 객실 서비스 규정에 따라 객실 수화물 선반(Overhead Bin)을 열어 육안으로 확인할 수 있다.
3. 객실 서비스 규정에 따라 코트 룸 및 승객 좌석 하단, 창측, 승객 좌석 주머니(Seat Pocket) 등을 육안으로 점검할 수 있다.
4. 객실 서비스 규정에 따라 유실물 발견 시 상급자에게 보고하고 승무원은 최대한 빨리 승객에게 인계할 수 있다.

1. Good job 잘했습니다, 수고하셨습니다

2. lost property 유실물

3. apart from ~외에도, 제외하고

4. loss 분실, 손실

5. Lost and Found 분실물 보관소

6. leather 가죽

7. pass on 넘겨주다

8. make a report 알리다, 접수하다

9. the ground floor 1층

Dialogue 9-1

Track 44

Checking for lost property

> A1 : Flight Attendant 1   A2 : Flight Attendant 2
> A3 : Flight Attendant 3   M : Cabin Manager   GS : Ground Staff

A1 : We haven't found anything in B/C

A2 : I've found a pair of glasses in the seat pocket of seat 28E in zone B.

A3 : Good job. There is no lost property in zone C.

M : Got it. Did you find anything apart from the pair of glasses?

A2 : No, nothing else.

M : Got it. (Talking to the ground staff on a walkie-talkie) We've found a pair of glasses in the seat pocket of 28E on flight SQ 607.[11]

GS : The passenger reported his lost glasses to the check-in desk. Please bring them to check-in desk number 2.

M : Copy.

---

11) SQ - Singapore Airline

Substitution Drill 9-1

Direction : Practice the conversation with your partner using the information given in the table below.

A1 : We haven't found anything in B/C

A2 : I've found (1) _____ in the seat pocket of seat

(2) _____ in zone B.

A3 : Good job. There is no lost property in zone C.

M : Got it. Did you find anything apart from (3) _____?

A2 : No, nothing else.

M : Got it. (Talking to the ground staff on a walkie-talkie) We've found

(1) _____ in the seat pocket of (2) _____ on flight

(4) _____.

GS : (5) _____.

M : Copy.

	(1) Found item	(2) Seat number	(3) Found item	(4) Flight number	(5) Status of report
A	a tablet PC	35C	the tablet	CX434[12]	There is no report of the loss yet. Please bring it to Lost and Found once you've disembarked
B	a pair of leather gloves	47B	the gloves	QR1312[13]	The passenger made a report for the loss of the gloves at Lost and Found. Would you pass on the gloves to the lost and found center?
C	a passport	55A	the passport	EK5123[14]	The passenger made a report to the airport police. Please come to the police station on the ground floor

12) CX - Cathay Pacific Airways
13) QR - Qatar Airway
14) EK - Emirates Airline

2) Checking for Remaining Passengers (잔류 승객 점검하기)

Objective Duties (학습 목표)

1. 객실 서비스 규정에 따라 밀폐 공간(화장실 및 벙커(Bunk)) 내 잔류 승객 여부를 점검할 수 있다.

2. 객실 서비스 규정에 따라 각각의 승무원은 담당 존 별로 결과를 구두로 보고할 수 있다.

3. 객실 서비스 규정에 따라 잔류 승객을 조치할 수 있다.

Words and Phrases (어휘와 어구)

1. remaining passenger 잔류 승객

2. stomachache 위통, 복통

3. sudden pain 갑작스런 통증

4. medical team 의료팀, 의료진

5. sickness 질병, 아픔

6. symptom 증상

7. cramp 경련(쥐)

8. cold 감기

9. suffer from ~로 고통 받다

10. headache 두통

Dialogue 9-2   Track 45

Checking for remaining passengers.

> A1 : Flight Attendant 1   A2 : Flight Attendant 2
> M : Cabin Manager   P : Passenger

A1 : There are no remaining passengers in zones D and E.

A2 : Not in zone C either.

A1 : There is one passenger sitting in seat 15D in zone B because she has a stomachache.

M : Got it. (Walking to the seat) Excuse me sir/ma'am. Are you all right? May I help you?

P : I felt a sudden pain in the stomach right after the airplane landed. It's hard to walk now.

M : Oh that's terrible. May I call a medical team?

P : No. I don't think that's necessary. I think I'll be all right soon.

M : Okay. We'll get a wheelchair for you. One of our ground crew will help you disembark. He/She'll also take you to the immigration and the baggage claim areas.

P : Thank you very much.

Substitution Drill 9-2

Direction : Practice the conversation with your partner using the information given in the table below.

A1 : There are no remaining passengers in zones D and E.

A2 : Not in zone C either.

A1 : There is one passenger sitting in seat (1) _____ in zone B

because (2) _____ .

M : Got it. (Walking to the seat) Excuse me sir/ma'am. Are you all right? May I

help you?

P : (3) _____ .

M : Oh that's terrible. May I call a medical team?

P : No. I don't think that's necessary. I think I'll be all right soon.

M : Okay. We'll get a wheelchair for you. One of our ground crew will

help you disembark. He/She'll also take you to the immigration and the

baggage claim areas.

P : Thank you very much.

	(1) Seat number	(2) Sickness	(3) Symptom
A	12C	he seems to have some pain in his leg	I have a cramp in my left leg. It's difficult to walk
B	10A	she has a terrible cold	My cold has got worse, but I think I can walk
C	22D	he's suffering from a terrible headache	I suddenly felt a pain in my head. I can't walk properly

3) Checking the Cabin Facilities and Equipment (기내 설비 점검하기)

 Objective Duties (학습 목표)

1. 객실 서비스 규정에 따라 객실 내 장착되어있는 모든 서비스 설비나 장비를 점검할 수 있다.

2. 객실 서비스 규정에 따라 객실 설비나 장비를 점검 후 이상 유무를 보고할 수 있다.

3. 객실 서비스 규정에 따라 객실 설비나 장비에 이상이 있을 경우 정비사에게 구두 전달하고 객실 설비 장비 수리 요청서에 기록할 수 있다.

Words and Phrases (어휘와 어구)

1. make a noise 소음을 낸다, 시끄럽게 하다

2. repair request form 수리요청서

3. do the repair 수리하다

4. loose 느슨한

Dialogue 9-3　　　　　　　　　　　　　　　　Track 46

Checking the cabin equipment and facilities.

MC : Maintenance Crew　　　A : Flight Attendant

MC : Were there any problems with the equipment or the facilities during the flight?

A : The button to recline seat 32G didn't work properly. And the lavatory door in front of the R2 door makes a little noise when it opens. Also, the temperature of the oven in the mid-galley doesn't go above 50°F.

MC : Okay. I've checked the repair request form and I'll do the repair now.

A : Thank you very much.

Substitution Drill 9-3

Direction : Practice the conversation with your partner using the information given in the table below.

MC : Were there any problems with the equipment or the facilities during the flight?

A :   (1) _____ . And (2) _____ .

Also, (3) _____ .

MC : Okay. I've checked the repair request form and I'll do the repair now.

A :   Thank you very much.

	(1) Problem 1	(2) Problem 2	(3) Problem 3
A	The tray of seat 38E is loose	the temperature of the refrigerator is too low	The lights above 45A, 52C, and 61D are a bit dim
B	The toilet in the lavatory in front of L2 door doesn't flush	the remote control of the VOD system for seat 34B doesn't work	The coffee maker is out of order
C	The lid of the overhead bin in zone C is too loose and doesn't click when it closes	The armrest in seat 47C doesn't go down	The water tap in the lavatory near L2 door doesn't work well

4) Handing over the In-flight Service Items (기내 용품 인계 · 인수하기)

 Objective Duties (학습 목표)

1. 객실 서비스 규정에 따라 기내에 탑재된 서비스용품 및 면세품을 컴파트먼트(Compartment)에 넣고 봉인(Sealing)할 수 있다.

2. 객실 서비스 규정에 따라 조리실(Galley) 담당자가 봉인(Sealing)한 후 인수인계서를 상호 점검할 수 있다.

3. 객실 서비스 규정에 따라 지상 종업원과 봉인 확인 및 점검(seal to seal) 방법으로 인계, 인수할 수 있다.

Words and Phrases (어휘와 어구)

1. handover form 인수인계서

2. seal 봉(인)하다

3. go over ~를 조사하다, 점검하다

4. seal 봉인, 인장

5. intact 온전한, 전혀 다치지 않은

6. tightly 단단히, 꽉

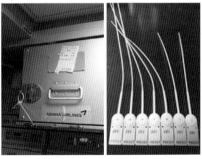

Picture 1 — Seal

Dialogue 9-4　　　　　　　　　　　　　　　Track ∘47

Handing over the in-flight service items

> A : Flight Attendant　　　CS : Catering Staff

A :　I've sealed the cart for the service items. Here is the handover form.

CS : Okay. Here is the form. Let's check the number together.

A :　Okay. Have you checked it? I'll sign here.

CS : Sure. I'll sign here too. Thank you very much.

Substitution Drill 9-4

Direction : Practice the conversation with your partner using the information given in the table below.

A : I've sealed the cart for (1) _____. Here is

the handover form.

CS : Okay. Here is the form. Let's (2) _____.

A : Okay. Have you checked it? I'll sign here.

CS : Sure. I'll sign here too. Thank you very much.

	(1) Items	(2) Confirming the sealing
A	the duty-free items	go over the form and check the seal
B	the liquor	make sure that the seal is intact
C	the giveaway items	check whether the cart is sealed tightly

Cabin Crew Management
객실 승무관리

1) Assigning Duties to Each Attendant (객실 승무원별 근무 배정하기)

 Objective Duties (학습 목표)

1. 객실 서비스 및 객실 안전 규정에 따라 객실 승무원에게 업무를 할당할 수 있다.

2. 효율적 서비스를 위해 노선 특성에 따라 객실 승무원별 업무 배정을 조정할 수 있다.

3. 효율적 서비스를 위해 객실 승무원의 역량을 고려하여 업무 배정을 조정할 수 있다.

Words and Phrases (어휘와 어구)

1. assign duties 업무를 배정하다

2. cabin briefing 기내브리핑(회의)

3. intranet(≠ internet) 내부전산망

4. go over ~를 점검하다, 검토하다

5. TS(travel class senior) 일반석 선임승무원

6. BL(zone B left side) B존의 왼쪽 편

7. BR(zone B right side) B존의 오른쪽 편

8. CL(zone C left side) C존의 왼쪽 편

9. CR(zone C right side) C존의 오른쪽 편

10. be well aware of 익히 알다

11. emergency safety equipment
    비상안전장비

12. take advance orders(pre-orders)
    사전주문을 받다

13. return flight back to
    ~로 돌아오는 비행 편

Picture 1 — A Pre-order Form of Qatar Airways

Dialogue 10-1   Track 48

Assigning duties to flight attendants (at the cabin briefing)

> M : Cabin Manager

M : How are you? I'm Sunhee Choi, the cabin manager today. You must have been informed of your duties through the intranet. However, I'd like to go over your duties once again. Ms. Jaesook Lee is B/C senior, Ms. Bora Kim is B/C galley, and Ms. Songhee Park is B/C junior. In Y/C, Ms. Jae-eun Song is TS[15], who is supposed to work at BL[16]. Ms. Nina Yoo, you're at BR[17] and you're in charge of the boarding greeting and door duty. Ms. Sumi Chun in CL[18] is in charge of the announcements. Ms. Jihye Kim is in charge of CR[19] and Mr. Jongsoo Lim is in charge of the duty-free items. I'd like all of you to be well aware of your assigned areas and check the emergency safety equipment. The attendant in charge of selling duty-free items must pay special attention when taking advance orders (pre-orders) for the return flight back to Korea. There might be many orders so please be careful not to make any mistakes. As you know flights to and from China have a lot of group passengers. An overseas Chinese attendant in CR will assist you if there are any complaints and if any problems occur. Enjoy the flight.

---

15) TS: T is for T/C (travel class), the term used for Y/C (economy class) by Korean Air. TS refers to travel class senior, in other words, economy class zone senior.
16) BL: zone B left side
17) BR: zone B right side
18) CL: zone C left side
19) CR: zone C right side

Substitution Drill 10-1

Direction : Practice the conversation with your partner using the information given in the table below.

M : How are you? I'm (1) _____, the cabin manager today. You must have been informed of your duties through the intranet. However, I'd like to go over your duties once again. (2) _____ is B/C senior, Ms. Bora Kim is B/C galley, and (3) _____ is B/C junior. In Y/C, Ms. Jae-eun Song is TS, who is supposed to work at BL. Ms. Nina Yoo, you're at BR and you're in charge of the boarding greeting and door duty. Ms. Sumi Chun in CL and is in charge of the announcements. Ms. Jihye Kim is in charge of CR and Mr. Jongsoo Lim is in charge of the duty-free items. I'd like all of you to be well aware of your assigned areas and check the emergency safety equipment. The attendant in charge of selling duty-free items must pay special attention when taking advance orders (pre-orders) for the return flight back to Korea. There might be many orders so please be careful not to make any mistakes. As you know flights to and from China have a lot of group passengers. An overseas Chinese attendant in CR will assist you if there are any complaints and if any problems occur. Enjoy the flight.

	(1) Your name	(2) B/C senior	(3) B/C junior
A	Your name	Your friend's name 1	Your friend's name 2
B	Your name	Your friend's name 3	Your friend's name 4
C	Your name	Your friend's name 5	Your friend's name 6

2) Sharing Information between the Cockpit and the Cabin Zones (운항 · 객실 간 정보 공유하기)

Objective Duties (학습 목표)

1. 객실 서비스 및 객실 안전 규정에 따라 객실 상황을 판단하여 상급자에게 신속하게 보고할 수 있다.

2. 객실 서비스 및 객실 안전 규정에 따라 운항 정보를 공유할 수 있다.

3. 객실 서비스 및 객실 안전 규정에 따라 승객 정보를 공유할 수 있다.

Words and Phrases (어휘와 어구)

1. **joint flight with** ~항공과 제휴(합동 비행)

2. **Pacific Time** 태평양 표준시

3. **F/C**(first class) 일등석

4. **B/C**(business class) 비즈니스석

5. **Y/C**(economy class) 일반석

6. **turbulence** 난기류

7. **ring** 울리다

8. **irregularities** 이상징후

9. **KST**(Korean Standard Time) 한국 표준시

Dialogue 10-2

Track 49

Briefing for flight

> P : Pilot   M : Cabin Manager

P : How are you? I'm the pilot of flight OZ202, Gipyo Kim. I'm glad to be flying with you. The flight OZ202 is a joint flight with AA7412 departing Seoul and flying to Los Angles in the USA. We will take off at 14:50 KST on December 25, 2015. The flight time will be 11 hours and 30 minutes. Our plane will arrive in Los Angeles at 10:20 Pacific Time on December 25, 2015. We have five F/C passengers, 28 B/C passengers, and 45 Y/C passengers today. We expect there will be some turbulence due to cloudy weather conditions. When the seat belt sign rings twice, all crew members must immediately sit down. As the cabin manager, you must report anything unusual that happens in the cabin.

M : Yes, sir/ma'am. I'll call you first before closing and opening the aircraft door. I'll also report any irregularities in the cabin. Today many transit passengers will board in the Philippines. If the connecting aircraft is delayed, I'll also let you know.

Substitution Drill 10-2

Direction : Practice the conversation with your partner using the information given in the table below.

P : How are you? I'm the pilot of flight OZ202, Gipyo Kim. I'm glad to be flying with you. The flight OZ202 is a joint flight with AA7412 departing Seoul and flying to (1) _____. We will take off at (2) _____. The flight time will be (3) _____. Our plane will arrive in (4) _____. We have five F/C passengers, 28 B/C passengers, and 45 Y/C passengers today. We expect there will be some turbulence due to cloudy weather conditions. When the seat belt sign rings twice, all crew members must immediately sit down. As the cabin manager, you must report anything unusual that happens in the cabin.

M : Yes, sir/ma'am. I'll call you first before closing and opening the aircraft door. I'll also report any irregularities in the cabin. Today many transit passengers will board in the Philippines. If the connecting aircraft is delayed, I'll also let you know.

	(1) Destination	(2) Departure time	(3) Flight time	(4) Arrival time
A	New York	16:30 KST on July 20	14 hours	New York at 17:30 on July 20
B	Bangkok	8:20 local time on August 11	5 hours and 55 minutes	Bangkok at 12:15 on August 11
C	Beijing	10:45 on May 28	2 hours and 15 minutes	Beijing at 12:00 on May 28

3) Handling Passengers with Complaints (불만 승객 대처하기)

 Objective Duties (학습 목표)

1. 객실 서비스 및 객실 안전 규정에 따라 불만 상황에 대한 원인을 파악할 수 있다.

2. 객실 서비스 및 객실 안전 규정에 따라 경청한 후 불만에 대한 해결 방안을 모색할 수 있다.

3. 객실 서비스 및 객실 안전 규정에 따라 해결방안에 대한 구체적인 행동을 보여줄 수 있다.

4. 객실 서비스 및 객실 안전 규정에 따라 해당 승객에 대한 만족도를 재확인할 수 있다.

Words and Phrases (어휘와 어구)

1. spill 쏟아지다, 엎지르다

2. annoyed 짜증이 난

3. stumble 넘어지다

4. wet tissue 물티슈

5. express one's deepest regret 머리 숙여 사과하다

6. pants 바지

7. stain 얼룩지게 하다, 더럽히다

8. cleaning coupon 세탁 쿠폰

9. worth ~의 가치가 있는

10. airline counter 항공사 카운터

11. on purpose 고의로, 일부러

Dialogue 10-3

Track 50

Handling passengers with complaints

> P : Passenger   A : Flight Attendant
> M : Cabin Manager

P : Argh! You just spilled juice on me!

A : Oh, I'm very sorry sir/ma'am. You must be so annoyed. Sudden turbulence caused me to stumble. I'm really sorry for this. Here is a wet tissue. May I help you?

P : No, I'll do that.

A : I really want to express my deepest regret. (The flight attendant should then report to the cabin manager, who will approach to the passenger.)

M : Excuse me, sir/ma'am. I'm the cabin manager, Sunhee Choi. I've heard that the attendant serving in this zone accidently spilled some juice on you. I'm very sorry for the trouble. How are your pants?

P : As you can see, the orange juice has stained my pants. I have a meeting right after arrival.

M : Oh I see. What an unfortunate situation! We have prepared a cleaning coupon worth 20,000 won for you. Please present this coupon at the airline counter when you arrive and use the money to clean your pants. I want to express my regret once again.

P : I guess it's all right. She didn't do it on purpose. It happened because of the turbulence. Thank you for the cleaning coupon.

M : I'm glad you understand. Thank you very much. If you have any other problems or complaints, please let us know.

Substitution Drill 10-3

Direction : Practice the conversation with your partner using the information given in the table below.

P : Argh! (1) _____!

A : Oh, I'm very sorry sir/ma'am. You must be so annoyed. Sudden turbulence caused me to stumble. I'm really sorry for this. Here is a wet tissue. May I help you?

P : No, I'll do that.

A : I really want to express my deepest regret. (The flight attendant should then report to the cabin manager, who will approach to the passenger.)

M : Excuse me, sir/ma'am. I'm the cabin manager, (2) _____. I've heard that the attendant serving in this zone accidently spilled some juice on you. I'm very sorry for the trouble. (3) _____.

P : As you can see, (4) _____. I have a meeting right after arrival.

M : Oh I see. What an unfortunate situation! We have prepared a cleaning coupon worth 20,000 won for you. Please present this coupon at the airline counter when you arrive and use the money to clean your (5) _____. I want to express my regret once again.

P : I guess it's all right. She didn't do it on purpose. It happened because of the turbulence. Thank you for the cleaning coupon.

M : I'm glad you understand. Thank you very much. If you have any other problems or complaints, please let us know.

	(1) Problem	(2) Name	(3) Checking the problem	(4) Complaint	(5) The clothes to be dry-cleaned
A	You just spilled juice all over my jacket	Your name	Let me see your jacket	My jacket is stained	jacket
B	You just stained my blouse	Your name	How is your blouse?	My white blouse has turned yellow	blouse
C	You just spilt water on my dress	Your name	May I take a look at your dress?	My dress is dirty	dress

4) Writing and Keeping Documents for Departure and Arrival (출 · 도착 서류작성 · 관리하기)

 Objective Duties (학습 목표)

1. 객실 서비스 및 객실 안전 규정에 따라 항공기 출발에 필요한 각종 서류의 수량, 종류 등을 점검할 수 있다.

2. 객실 서비스 및 객실 안전 규정에 따라 도착지 국가별 요구사항에 따라 입국에 필요한 서류를 요청할 수 있다.

3. 비행 중 발생한 기내 안전 및 서비스 설비에 대한 특이사항을 기록할 수 있다.

4. 항공기 도착 전 지상직원에게 인계해줄 서류의 이상 유무를 점검할 수 있다.

5. 항공기 도착 시 지상직원에게 객실 운항 관련 서류를 인계할 수 있다.

5) Managing Cabin Services (객실 서비스 관리하기)

Objective Duties (학습 목표)

1. 승무원 근무 규정에 따라 스페셜 식사는 객실 사무장이 직접 제공하면서 오전달이나 누락이 발생하지 않도록 재확인할 수 있다.

2. 객실 서비스 규정에 따라 비행 중 기내 질서유지 및 쾌적한 휴식환경 조성을 위해 단체 승객에 의한 소란, 소음 등을 항시 점검할 수 있다.

3. 객실 서비스 규정에 의해 화장실 청결 상태를 확인하며 비행 중에 발생할 수 있는 안전과 환자 발생에 대한 안전사항을 점검할 수 있다.

4. 승무원 근무 규정에 따라 기내 소음에 대한 관리를 할 수 있다.

5. 조리실(Galley) 내에서 작업 시, 통로(Aisle)를 걸어 다닐 때 승무원들 간의 대화, 컴파트먼트(Compartment), 카트(Cart), 캐리어박스(carrier box) 등의 문을 열고 닫을 때 객실 수화물 선반(Overhead Bin)의 손잡이를 열고 닫을 때 등 승무원을 관리 감독할 수 있다.

Words and Phrases (어휘와 어구)

1. catch up on 만회하다, 따라잡다

2. lower voice 목소리를 낮추다

3. excited 신이 난, 들뜬

4. complain of ~에 대해 하소연하다, 불평하다

5. take extra care 특별히 주의하다

6. snack 간식

Dialogue 10-5-1　　　　　　　　　　　　　　　　　Track 51

Controlling the noise made by a group of passengers.

> P1 : Passenger 1 　　　A : Flight Attendant
>
> P2 : Passenger 2 　　　M : Cabin Manager

P1 : I can't sleep because the passengers behind me are making too much noise. Most of the other passengers are asleep. Could you do something for me?

A : Certainly, sir/ma'am.

> (The attendant should walk around for a while in the area
> to confirm that the noise level is too high.)

A : Excuse me. Are you and your friend having a nice flight?

P2 : Yes, we're having a great flight. We haven't seen each other for a long time so we've been catching up on a lot of things.

A : Oh, I see. You must be really happy traveling with your friend. Sorry to say this but it is one in the morning in the city we departed from. Therefore most of the passengers are asleep. Some passengers can't sleep because you are talking too loud. Could you please lower your voice or move to the back of the cabin to talk with your friend?

P2 : Oh, I didn't realize that. I'm very sorry for the noise. We were just about to take a rest now anyway.

M : Thank you for understanding.

Substitution Drill 10-5-1

Direction : Practice the conversation with your partner using the information given in the table below.

P1 : I can't sleep because the passengers behind me are making too much noise. Most of the other passengers are asleep. Could you do something for me?

A : Certainly, sir/ma'am.

       (The attendant should walk around for a while in the area
       to confirm that the noise level is too high.)

A : Excuse me. Are you and your (1) _____ having a nice flight?

P2 : Yes, we're having a great flight. (2) _____.

A : Oh, I see. You must be really happy traveling with your (1) _____.
Sorry to say this but it is one in the morning in the city we departed from. Therefore most of the passengers are asleep. Some passengers can't sleep because you are talking too loud. Could you please lower your voice or move to the back of the cabin to talk with your (1) _____?

P2 : Oh, I didn't realize that. I'm very sorry for the noise. We were just about to take a rest now anyway.

M : Thank you for understanding.

	(1) Companion	(2) Reason for not sleeping
A	sisters	this is the first time for me to travel with my sisters and we're really excited
B	family	this is our first overseas trip so we're really excited
C	parents	we haven't travelled for a long time so we're really excited about our trip

Dialogue 10-5-2   Track 52

Dealing with the noise in the galley.

> M : Cabin Manager   A : Flight Attendant

M : Thanks for working so hard. You must be preparing the second meal.

A : Yes, we are putting the second entrée in the oven.

M : Right. The cabin lights are all off and most of the passengers are asleep. When you prepare the service, please make sure that you don't make any noise. The passengers near the galley are complaining of the lights coming from the galley because the curtain is not closed tightly enough. Please take extra care when the passengers are asleep.

A : Okay. We will be extremely careful not to make any noise.

Substitution Drill 10-5-2

Direction : **Practice the conversation with your partner using the information given in the table below.**

M : Thanks for working so hard. You must be preparing (1) _____.

A : Yes, (2) _____.

M : Right. The cabin lights are all off and most of the passengers are asleep. When you prepare the service, please make sure that you don't make any noise. The passengers near the galley are complaining of the lights coming from the galley because the curtain is not closed tightly enough. Please take extra care when the passengers are asleep.

A : Okay. We will be extremely careful not to make any noise.

	(1) Meal service	(2) Preparation process
A	dinner	we are heating the main entrées
B	breakfast	we are taking out the entrées out of the oven
C	snack	we are making sure there are enough snacks for the passengers

Flight Safety
항공 안전

Cabin Safety Management
기내 안전관리

1) Checking Safety and Security before Boarding
(승객탑승 전 안전 · 보안 점검하기)

 Objective Duties (학습 목표)

1. 항공기 안전 규정에 따라 승객 탑승 전, 항공기 객실의 안전장비 점검할 수 있다.

2. 항공기 안전 규정에 따라 승객 탑승 전, 항공기 객실의 보안장비 점검할 수 있다.

3. 항공기 안전 규정에 따라 승객 탑승 전, 항공기 안전 운항에 관계되는 의심스러운 물건에 대하여 신속히 보고할 수 있다.

4. 항공기 안전 규정에 따라 기내 작업 인력에 대한 동향을 파악하여, 이상 발생 시, 보고할 수 있다.

1. pre-flight check 승객탑승 전 안전 · 보안 점검

2. O_2 bottle 산소 병

3. gauge 게이지, 측정기

4. H_2O extinguisher 물 소화기

5. ripped off 떼어낸

6. explosion resistant blanket 폭발저항력이 있는 담요, 방폭 담요

7. emergency security equipment 비상안전장비

8. circuit breaker 회로 차단기

9. pop out 튀어 오르다

10. have ~ fixed ~을 수리하다

11. removed 제거된

12. flicker 깜박거리다

13. charged 충전된

14. explosion proof blanket 방폭 담요

15. trash bin hatch 쓰레기통 뚜껑, 투입구

16. megaphone 메가폰, 확성기

17. halon extinguisher 할론(탄소와 할로겐으로 구성된) 소화기

18. extinguishing agent 소화기 촉매제

19. life vest 구명 조끼

20. crash axe 사고 시 사용되는 도끼

Dialogue 11-1 Track 53

Pre-flight check (PA conversation)

> M : Cabin Manager
> A-F/C : Flight Attendant in Charge of First Class
> A-B/C : Flight Attendant in Charge of Business Class
> A-Y/C-B : Flight Attendant in Charge of Zone B in Economy Class
> A-Y/C-C : Flight Attendant in Charge of Zone C in Economy Class

M : Would you please report the results of the pre-flight check?

A-F/C : The emergency security equipment in F/C is OK.

A-B/C : The O_2 bottle gauge in B/C is showing that it's not full. It needs to be replaced. Everything else is fine.

A-Y/C-B : The H_2O extinguisher seal in zone B has been ripped off, and the explosion resistant blanket is missing. Everything else is OK with the emergency security equipment.

A-Y/C-C : The circuit breaker in the back galley has popped out. Would you please do something about it? Everything is OK with the rest of the emergency security equipment.

M : Okay, got it. I'll report to the cabin maintenance staff and have everything fixed. Please let me know when these problems have been fixed. Thank you.

Substitution Drill 11-1

Direction : Practice the conversation with your partner using the information given in the table below.

M :   Would you please report the results of the pre-flight check?

A-F/C :   The emergency security equipment in F/C is OK.

A-B/C :   (1) _____. It needs to be replaced. Everything else is fine.

A-Y/C-B : (2) _____, and (3) _____. Everything else is OK with the emergency security equipment.

A-Y/C-C : (4) _____. Would you please do something about it? Everything is OK with the rest of the emergency security equipment.

M :   Okay, got it. I'll report to the cabin maintenance staff and have everything fixed. Please let me know when these problems have been fixed. Thank you.

	(1) Problem 1	(2) Problem 2	(3) Problem 3	(4) Problem 4
A	The seal of the H_2O extinguisher in B/C has been removed	The green light of the flash light isn't flickering meaning it's not charged.	I can't find any explosion proof blankets	One of the four temperature indicators inside the trash bin is black
B	The trash bin hatch in the lavatory in front of R2 isn't working properly	I can't find any megaphones	There aren't enough explosion proof blankets	The galley circuit breaker in the middle of the cabin has popped out
C	The gauge of the halon extinguisher is lower than it should be	There is not enough extinguishing agent in one of the fire extinguishers in zone B	Two life vests are missing in seat 32C and 41D in zone B	A crash axe is not in its place

2) Checking Safety and Security of the Cabin before Departure and Arrival (항공기 이 · 착륙 전 안전 · 보안 관리하기)

Objective Duties (학습 목표)

1. 객실 안전 규정에 따라 승객에게 좌석 벨트 착용 안내를 정확하게 할 수 있다.

2. 객실 안전 규정에 따라 미 착석 승객을 확인하고, 착석을 유도할 수 있다.

3. 객실 안전 규정에 따라 객실 수화물 선반(Overhead Bin) 잠금 상태를 확인하고, 조치할 수 있다.

4. 객실 안전 규정에 따라 설비 잠금 상태를 확인하고, 조치할 수 있다.

5. 객실 안전 규정에 따라 비상시 관련 정보를 제공할 수 있다.

6. 객실 안전 규정에 따라 해당 항공기 문 Slide 상태를 비상 상태(Automatic Position)로 변경할 수 있다.

7. 객실 안전 규정에 따라 비상구 위치에 착석한 승객에게 비상시 행동 요령과 업무 협조를 안내할 수 있다.

8. 객실 안전 규정에 따라 창문 덮개(Window Shade)를 원위치 하도록 안내할 수 있다.

9. 객실 안전 규정에 따라 좌석 등받이와 좌석 앞 선반(Tray Table)을 원위치 하도록 안내할 수 있다.

10. 객실 안전 규정에 따라 좌석벨트 착용을 확인하고 점검할 수 있다.

11. 객실 안전 규정에 따라 비상 시 탈출 요령에 대한 절차를 이미지 트레이닝 할 수 있다.(Image Training)

12. 객실 안전 규정에 따라 항공기 탑승 후 다시 하기를 원하는 승객에 대하여 신속히 보고 할 수 있다.

13. 객실 안전 규정에 따라 의심스러운 승객 또는 돌발 상황에 대해 선임자에게 보고할 수 있다.

14. 객실 안전 규정에 따라 승객에게 전자기기 사용 금지 안내 방송을 하고, 조치할 수 있다.

 Words and Phrases (어휘와 어구)

1. do some stretches 스트레칭 하다, 기지개를 켜다

2. hurt oneself ~자신을 다치게 하다, 다치다

3. leave one's seatbelt unfastened ~의 안전벨트를 매지 않은 채로 두다, 안전벨트를 매지 않다

4. abide by the rule 규칙을 지키다

5. backache 허리통, 요통

6. leave ~ closed ~을 닫친 채로 놔두다

7. allocate 할당하다, 배정하다

8. give ~ a helping hand ~를 도와주다

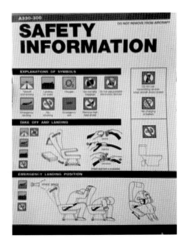

Picture 1 — Safety Instruction Card

Dialogue 11-2-1   Track 54

Opening window shades, returning tray tables to their original positions, returning seats to their upright position.

A : Flight Attendant   P : Passenger

A : Would you please fasten your seatbelt?

P : Okay, I'll fasten it. But why can't I leave it unfastened? I want to do some stretches while sitting in my seat.

A : You might hurt yourself during departure and landing if you leave your seatbelt unfastened.

P : Okay. Got it.

Substitution Drill 11-2-1

Direction : Practice the conversation with your partner using the information given in the table below.

A : Would you please (1) _____ ?

P : Okay, I'll (2) _____ . But, why can't I (3) _____ ?

    (4) _____ .

A : (5) _____ .

P : Okay. Got it.

	(1) Asking passenger what to do	(2) What passenger will do	(3) Com-plaining	(4) Reason for complaint	(5) Reason for abiding by the rule
A	return your seat to its upright position	return my seat	recline it	I have a terrible backache	It might hurt other passengers when evacuating in an emergency
B	return your tray table to its original position	return it to its original place	use it	I have to fill out this form	I understand it must be inconvenient for you, but it may harm others in an emergency evacuation
C	open the window shade	open it	leave it closed	There is too much sunshine coming in	Windows are used to find out what's going on outside in an emergency

Dialogue 11-2-2

Track 55

Guiding the passengers sitting near the exit - Part 1

> A : Flight Attendant P : Passenger

A : Excuse me, sir/ma'am. How are you? Are you traveling with children?

P : Yes.

A : May I check your boarding passes?

P : Sure. Is there anything wrong with our seats?

A : These seats are for those passengers who can help evacuate other passengers in an emergency. I'm very sorry to tell you this, but children cannot sit here.

P : Here are our boarding passes.

A : Thank you very much for your cooperation. Your seat numbers are correct. But I guess there has been a mistake allocating your seats. I'll show you to other seats after checking with the ground staff.

P : No problem.

A : (After a while) Thank you so much for waiting. I've found out there was an error in allocating your seats due to a problem in the system. Your seats are 37 C, D and E. I'm really sorry about the confusion.

P : What should I do with the bag I've put in the overhead bin?

A : We'll put it in the overhead bin above your new seats.

Substitution Drill 11-2-2

Direction : Practice the conversation with your partner using the information given in the table below.

A : Excuse me, sir/ma'am. How are you? Are you traveling with (1) _____?

P : Yes.

A : May I check your boarding passes?

P : Sure. Is there anything wrong with our seats?

A : These seats are for those passengers who can help evacuate other passengers in an emergency. I'm very sorry to tell you this, but (2) _____.

P : Here are our boarding passes.

A : Thank you very much for your cooperation. Your seat numbers are correct. But I guess there has been a mistake allocating your seats. I'll show you to other seats after checking with the ground staff.

P : No problem.

A : (After a while) Thank you so much for waiting. I've found out there was an error in allocating your seats due to a problem in the system. (3) _____. I'm really sorry about the confusion.

P : What should I do with the bag I've put in the overhead bin?

A : We'll put it in the overhead bin above your new seats.

	(1) Weak, disabled, and/or minor	(2) Passenger not allowed to sit near the exit	(3) Newly assigned seats
A	a baby	passengers' with babies cannot sit here	You and your husband are assigned to 43A and B
B	a child	passengers' with children are not allowed to sit here	Your seats are 31A and B
C	your grandmother	elderly and disabled passengers cannot sit in this area	You're assigned to seat 42B and C

Dialogue 11-2-3   Track 56

Guiding the passengers sitting near the exit - Part 2

A : Flight Attendant   P : Passenger

A : How are you? May I give you some information?

P : Sure.

A : This seat is right next to the emergency exit. The passenger sitting here must evacuate first and help others evacuate.

P : Okay. What do I have to do?

A : Please read the information card on emergency evacuations located in the pocket in front of you. As soon as this door opens in an emergency, you must evacuate and help others evacuate fast and smoothly at the bottom of the slide.

P : Okay, got it.

A : In addition, you mustn't place belongings on the floor during landing and departing. I'll put all your bags in the overhead bin.

P : Thank you.

Substitution Drill 11-2-3

Direction : Practice the conversation with your partner using the information given in the table below.

A : How are you? May I give you some information?

P : Sure.

A : (1) _____. The passenger sitting here must evacuate first and help others evacuate.

P : Okay. What do I have to do?

A : Please read the information card on emergency evacuations located in
the pocket in front of you. As soon as this door opens in an emergency,
(2) _____.

P : Okay, got it.

A : In addition, you mustn't place belongings on the floor during landing and
departing. I'll put all your bags in the overhead bin.

P : Thank you.

	(1) Location of seats	(2) what to do in an emergency
A	This seat is near the emergency exit	you have to help others evacuate
B	The seats are in the row next to the emergency exit	you have to slide down first and then help others at the bottom of the slide so that everyone can escape quickly and safely
C	These seats are near the emergency exit	you must get off first and give other passengers a helping hand at the bottom of the slide

3) Checking Safety and Security of the Cabin during the Flight (비행 중 안전 · 보안 관리하기)

 Objective Duties (학습 목표)

1. 객실 안전 규정에 따라 승객에게 상시 벨트 착용 여부를 확인하고, 안내를 할 수 있다.

2. 객실 안전 규정에 따라 승객의 기내 흡연 여부를 확인하고 제지할 수 있다.

3. 객실 안전 규정에 따라 밀폐 공간 내부 상태를 확인하여, 조치할 수 있다.

4. 객실 안전 규정에 따라 항공기 운항 중 행동이 의심스러운 승객의 동태 및 이상 물건에 대하여 신속히 보고할 수 있다.

5. 객실 안전 규정에 따라 난기류(Turbulence) 발생 시 승객에게 안내 방송을 하고, 필요 조치를 할 수 있다.

Picture 2 — Smoke Detector

Words and Phrases (어휘와 어구)

1. crew rest area 승무원 휴식 공간

2. handle 손잡이

3. off limits 출입금지

4. activate 작동시키다, 활성화시키다

5. smoke detector 연기 탐지기

6. cause 일으키다, 야기하다

7. sound 울리다

8. knock on ~를 두드리다

9. expression 표현

10. embarrassment 당혹감 쑥스러움

11. strictly 엄격하게

12. violate 어기다

13. prosecuted 기소된, 고소된

14. ember 불씨

15. banned 금지된

16. comply with this regulation 이 규칙을 따르다

17. illegal 불법의

18. subject to the non-smoking rule 금연규칙의 적용을 받다

Dialogue 11-3-1   Track 57

Checking inside crew rest area and stopping passengers smoking.

P : Passenger   A : Flight Attendant

P : Oh, what is this door for? There are some stairs. Is this a lavatory?

A : (Looking at the passenger) Excuse me, sir/ma'am. Please don't go in there.

P : I just opened it because there is a handle.

A : I'm sorry, sir/ma'am but that area is off limits to passengers.

P : Is there any space where I can smoke?

A : Of course not. The aircraft is a non-smoking area. In-flight smoking is prohibited by law.

P : Okay, got it.

Substitution Drill 11-3-1

Direction : Practice the conversation with your partner using the information given in the table below.

P : Oh, what is this door for? (1) _____?

A : (Looking at the passenger) Excuse me, sir/ma'am! Please don't go in there.

P : (2) _____.

A : I'm sorry, sir/ma'am but that area is off limits to passengers.

P : Is there any space where I can smoke?

A : Of course not. The aircraft is a non-smoking area. In-flight smoking is prohibited by law.

P : Okay, got it.

	(1) An enclosed area	(2) Reason for opening
A	Is this a closet	It looks like a smoking area
B	Is this an empty space	I was just curious to find out what it is for
C	Is this a rest area	I was wondering if I could rest inside

Dialogue 11-3-2   Track 58

Checking in-flight smoking

A : Flight Attendant   P : Passenger

(Smoke has activated a smoke detector causing the alarm to sound.)

A : (Knocking on the lavatory door very loudly) What's going on in there?

P : (A passenger opening the door with an expression of embarrassment) I only smoked one cigarette, but the alarm went off...

A : Smoking inside the aircraft is strictly prohibited. Passengers violating this law can be prosecuted under international aviation law.

P : Okay.

A : (The flight attendant checks the smoke detector, takes a look around inside the lavatory, checks inside the garbage can for any embers, and then reports to the cabin manager.)

** A flight attendant should respond very strongly in this event.

Substitution Drill 11-3-2

Direction : Practice the conversation with your partner using the information given in the table below.

(Smoke has activated a smoke detector causing the alarm to sound.)

A : (Knocking on the lavatory door very loudly) (1) _____?

P : (A passenger opening the door with an expression of embarrassment) I only smoked one cigarette, but the alarm went off...

A : (2) _____. (3) _____.

P : Okay.

A : (The flight attendant checks the smoke detector, takes a look around inside the lavatory, checks inside the garbage can for any embers, and then reports to the cabin manager.)

	(1) Checking inside the lavatory	(2) Smoking ban	(3) Asking passenger to obey the rule
A	Is anyone there	Smoking is banned anywhere in the aircraft	You must comply with this regulation
B	Who's inside	Smoking is not allowed while you're aboard	You must follow the rule
C	What are you doing in there	Smoking is illegal	Could you please understand that you are subject to the non-smoking rule

4) Checking Safety and Security after Landing
(착륙 후 안전 · 보안 점검 · 관리하기)

Objective Duties (학습 목표)

1. 객실 안전 규정에 따라 이동 승객을 제지하고, 착석상태 유지를 안내할 수 있다.

2. 객실 안전 규정에 따라 승객의 유실물을 점검하고, 조치할 수 있다.

3. 객실 안전 규정에 따라 기내 설비 이상 유무를 점검하고, 보고할 수 있다.

Words and Phrases (어휘와 어구)

1. **post-flight check** 착륙 후 안전 · 보안 점검관리

2. **taxiing** 비행기가 지상에서 천천히 주행하는 것

3. **line up** 줄을 서다

4. **flashlight** 손전등

5. **ELT**(emergency locator transmitter) 항공기용 구명 무선기

6. **PBE**(protective breathing equipment) 보호 호흡 장비

7. **AED**(automated external defibrillator) 자동 제세동기

8. **FAK**(first aid kit) 구급 상자

9. **pocket mask** 응급구조를 하는 승무원의 입에 쓰는 마스크

Dialogue 11-4   Track 59

Post-flight check.

P1 : Passenger   A : Flight Attendant   P2 : Passenger 2

(As the aircraft is taxiing after landing)

P1 : (Moving to the lavatory)

A : Excuse me sir/ma'am, you must remain seated while the aircraft is taxiing due to safety concerns.

P1 : Oh, okay. Sorry.

P2 : We've almost arrived. I'm just going to take out my stuff because I want to get off first (standing to take out his/her luggage).

A : Excuse me. You must remain in your seat while the aircraft is taxiing.

P2 : I'm only taking out my baggage.

A : (Adamantly) Please, sit down sir/ma'am. It is dangerous to move around while the aircraft is taxiing.

Substitution Drill 11-4

Direction : Practice the conversation with your partner using the information given in the table below.

(As the aircraft is taxiing after landing)

P1 : (Moving to the lavatory)

A : Excuse me sir/ma'am, you must remain seated while the aircraft is taxiing due to safety concerns.

P1 : Oh, okay. Sorry.

P2 : We've almost arrived. I'm just going to (1) ＿＿＿＿＿＿＿ (standing to take out his/her luggage).

A : Excuse me. You must remain in your seat while the aircraft is taxiing.

P2 : (2) ＿＿＿＿＿＿＿＿＿＿＿＿＿＿.

A : (Adamantly) Please, sit down sir/ma'am. It is dangerous to move around while the aircraft is taxiing.

	(1) Intended action	(2) The reason for doing so
A	go to the lavatory	I can't hold on
B	put on my jacket	I'm running out of time
C	line up at the front	I have a meeting in about 30 minutes

List of Emergency Safety and Security Equipment

When checking safety and security before boarding (pre-flight check), flight attendants have to check the following items.

Items	Usages
H₂O extinguisher	Used to extinguish burning clothes or paper. A flight attendant has to check whether it is sealed during the pre-flight check.
Halon extinguisher	Used to extinguish all kinds of fires such as when electrical equipment (oven, cabin lights, etc.) is on fire as well as volatile liquids. A flight attendant has to check its gauge and seal during the pre-flight check.
O₂ bottle	Used to provide O₂ to any passengers who need O₂ as well as to the cabin crew members and passengers in an emergency. A flight attendant has to check the gauges and seals during the pre-flight check.
Flashlight	Used to guide passengers to an exit in an emergency and for illumination at night during an emergency evacuation. It is attached underneath a flight attendants' jump seat. During the pre-flight check, a flight attendant has to check that the green light is flashing to indicate it is charged.
Megaphone	Used by flight attendants to communicate with passengers during an emergency evacuation. During the pre-flight check a flight attendant has to check whether it works by pressing the button and testing whether it makes a click sound.

Items	Usages
ELT	ELT stands for emergency locator transmitter. It transmits the location of an aircraft that has landed on the ground or on water and is used by rescue crews to locate the aircraft and/or passengers in the event of an emergency. A flight attendant has to check whether it is located in its right place during the pre-flight check.
PBE	PBE stands for protective breathing equipment. It is used to protect the wearer's face, prevent the inhalation of smoke and toxic gas during a fire in the cabin, and to enable the wearer to see. A flight attendant has to check whether it is located in its right place during the pre-flight check.
AED	AED stands for automated external defibrillator. It is used for a patient who is suffering from a sudden respiratory arrest or cardiac arrest during flight. A flight attendant has to check whether it is located in its right place during the pre-flight check.
Crash axe	Used to make an opening, perhaps in order to use a fire extinguisher in an otherwise unreachable location, or to access the cargo hold. A flight attendant has to check whether it is located in its right place during the pre-flight check.
FAK	FAK stands for first aid kit. It is a box of emergency medicine equipment which contains digestive medicine, antidiarrheal agents, sterilizers, nitroglycerin, etc. and is located in the cabin. When a flight attendant has to use it, he/she has to remove the seal. After using it, he/she has to record what has been used. A flight attendant has to check whether it is located in its right place during the pre-flight check. He/She also has to have a used FAK replaced with a new one.

Items	Usages
Medical kit	This contains surgical instruments for simple surgical procedures and can only be used by a doctor. It contains a blood pressure gauge, a stethoscope, surgical knives, etc. It is made by Banyan Co. and is often called a Banyan Kit. A flight attendant has to check whether it is located in its right place during the pre-flight check.
Pocket mask	Used to cover the mouth of a person administering rescue breathing. A flight attendant has to check whether it is located in its right place during the pre-flight check.

Additional Information 2

In-flight Announcement on Turbulence

Excerpted from : Asiana Airlines Announcement Passages

Ladies and gentlemen

1. We will be passing through an area of turbulence.

2. We are now passing through an area of turbulence.

Please return to your seat and fasten your seat belt.

(For suspending service)

Also, we will be suspending the beverage service.

The service will be continued as soon as conditions improve.

Thank you.

Dealing with a Medical Emergency
응급환자 대처

---

1) Checking and Reporting an Occurrence of a Medical Emergency (응급환자 발생상황 파악 · 보고하기)

 Objective Duties (학습 목표)

1. 객실 서비스 및 객실 안전 규정에 따라 기내 환자 발생 여부를 파악할 수 있다.

2. 객실 서비스 및 객실 안전 규정에 따라 환자에 대한 정보를 신속하게 상급자에게 보고할 수 있다.

3. 객실 서비스 및 객실 안전 규정에 따라 환자에 대한 정보를 공유하도록 할 수 있다.

 Words and Phrases (어휘와 어구)

1. occurrence 발생

2. have trouble breathing 숨쉬기가 어렵다

3. feel pressure 부담감을 느끼다

4. chest 가슴

5. oxygen mask 산소마스크

6. treat A with B A에게 B를 가지고 처치하다

7. page a doctor 의사를 찾다

8. keep A up to date A에게 최신의 소식을 알리다

9. diagnosed 진단받다

10. emergency landing permit 비상착륙허가

11. alternate airport 대체 공항

12. conduct walk-around services 순회 서비스를 하다

13. reassure 안심시키다

14. set A at ease A를 안정시키다

Dialogue 12-1

Track 60

Checking and reporting occurrence of a medical emergency:

P1 : Passenger 1   A1 : Flight Attendant 1   P2 : Passenger 2
A2 : Flight Attendant 2   M : Cabin Manager   PT : Pilot

P1 : Excuse me, miss, the passenger next to me seems to be having trouble breathing.

A1 : Excuse me, sir/ma'am. Are you all right? Can you breathe?

P2 : Suddenly I'm finding it difficult to breathe, and I feel pressure in my chest. I need an oxygen mask, please.

A1 : Have you used the oxygen mask before?

P2 : Yeah.

A1 : (to Flight Attendant 2) Would you please bring me an O_2 bottle? And please let the cabin manager know about this situation.

A2 : Okay. I will. (After a while) Here is an O_2 bottle. You can use this. (To the cabin manager) The passenger in 37B feels a pain in his chest and is having some difficulties breathing. The attendant, Jung-Ah Kim, is treating the passenger with an O_2 bottle.

M : Okay. Please page a doctor. (On an interphone) Captain Stevenson, I'm calling to let you know that we have an emergency medical situation. The passenger in 37B is having trouble breathing and is being treated with an O_2 bottle. We're paging a doctor right now.

PT : Okay. Please keep me up to date. If it's a serious emergency as diagnosed by a doctor, please let me know immediately. I'll have to get an emergency landing permit from an alternate airport.

M : Okay. (To Flight Attendant 2) Please let the other attendants know about this situation and ask them to conduct walk-around services to reassure the other passengers.

A2 : Sure.

Substitution Drill 12-1

Direction : Practice the conversation with your partner using the information given in the table below.

P1 : Excuse me, miss, the passenger next to me seems to be having trouble breathing.

A1 : Excuse me, sir/ma'am. Are you all right? Can you breathe?

P2 : Suddenly I'm finding it difficult to breathe, and I feel pressure in my chest. I need an oxygen mask, please.

A1 : Have you used the oxygen mask before?

P2 : Yeah.

A1 : (to Flight Attendant 2) Would you please bring me an O_2 bottle? And please let the cabin manager know about this situation.

A2 : Okay. I will. (After a while) Here is an O_2 bottle. You can use this. (To the cabin manager) The passenger in (1) _____ feels a pain in his chest and is having some difficulties breathing. The attendant, (2) _____, is treating the passenger with an O_2 bottle.

M : Okay. Please page a doctor. (On an interphone) Captain Stevenson, I'm calling to let you know that we have an emergency medical situation. The passenger in (1) _____ is having trouble breathing and is being treated with an O_2 bottle. We're paging a doctor right now.

PT : Okay. Please keep me up to date. If it's a serious emergency as diagnosed by a doctor, please let me know immediately. I'll have to get an emergency landing permit from an alternate airport.

M : Okay. (To Flight Attendant 2) Please let the other attendants know about this situation and (3) _____.

A2 : Sure.

	(1) Seat number	(2) Name of A1	(3) How to calm down other passengers
A	55A	Name of A1	ask them to set other passengers at ease
B	10C	Name of A1	have them explain the situation to the other passengers as they walk around the cabin
C	36D	Name of A1	have them reassure the other passengers and answer any questions

2) Initial Response to a Medical Emergency (응급환자 초기 대응하기)

 Objective Duties (학습 목표)

1. 객실 서비스 및 객실 안전 규정에 따라 응급 처치할 수 있다.

2. 객실 서비스 및 객실 안전 규정에 따라 환자의 응급 상태를 확인하고 탑승 의사와 의료진을 신속하게 찾을 수 있다.

3. 객실 서비스 및 객실 안전 규정에 따라 응급 치료 장비를 탑승 의사의 협조를 구해 활용할 수 있도록 조치할 수 있다.

 Words and Phrases (어휘와 어구)

1. initial response 초기 대응

2. Banyan Kit 반얀키트(반얀이라는 회사에서 제조한 비상용 의료장비 키트)

3. nitroglycerine 니트로글리세린

4. try rescue breathing 구조 호흡을 시도하다

5. thermometer 온도계, 체온계

6. scissors 가위

7. bind up 붕대로 매다

8. wound 상처

9. abdominal pad 복부용 패드

10. bleeding 출혈

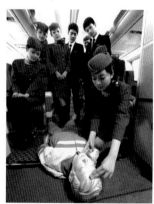

Picture 1 — A Flight Attendant Demonstrating Giving First Aid

Example Announcement

Excerpted from : Korean Air Announcement for Paging for Doctors and Nurses

May I have your attention, please? We have a medical situation on board. If there's a doctor or anyone with medical training on board, please contact a flight attendant immediately. Thank you.

Picture 2 — First Aid Kit

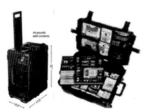

Picture 3 — Banyan Kit

Dialogue 12-2   Track ∘ 61

Initial response to a medical emergency.

D : Doctor   A : Flight Attendant

D : Do you have any medical equipment we could use?

A : Yes, we have a Banyan Kit, a first aid kit, and an AED (automated external defibrillator).

D : Could you bring them all?

A : Sure.

D : Do you have any nitroglycerine?

A : Yes, it's in the first aid kit.

D : Okay. I'm going to try rescue breathing and then use the AED.

A : Let me know what I can do to help.

Picture 4 — AED

Substitution Drill 12-2

Direction : Practice the conversation with your partner using the information given in the table below.

D : Do you have any medical equipment we could use?

A : Yes, we have a Banyan Kit, a first aid kit, and an AED (automated external defibrillator).

D : Could you bring them all?

A : Sure.

D : Do you have (1) _____?

A : Yes, it's/they're in the (2) _____.

D : Okay. (3) _____ and then use the AED.

A : Let me know what I can do to help.

	(1) Medical equipment	(2) Kit	(3) What to do
A	a thermometer	the first aid kit	Let me check his/ her temperature first
B	a pair of scissors	the Banyan Kit	First, I'll bind up his wound
C	an abdominal pad	the first aid kit	I'll have to stop the bleeding

3) Subsequent Management of a Medical Emergency
(응급환자 후속 관리하기)

 Objective Duties (학습 목표)

1. 응급환자 대응매뉴얼에 따라 응급환자 상태가 악화되지 않도록 관리할 수 있다.

2. 응급환자 발생에 따라 일반 탑승자의 쾌적한 여행이 방해되지 않도록 조치할 수 있다.

3. 착륙 후 응급환자 대응매뉴얼에 따라 공항과의 협조체제가 순조롭게 진행될 수 있게 조치할 수 있다.

Words and Phrases (어휘와 어구)

1. subsequent management 후속 관리

2. follow-up measure 후속 조치

3. medic 의사, 위생병

4. offer treatment 처치를 제공하다

5. on board 선상에

6. as planned 계획된대로

7. concern 관심, 걱정

8. surgeon 외과 의사

Dialogue 12-3-1   Track 62

Subsequent management of a medical emergency.

> A : Flight Attendant   SP : Sick Passenger

A : Excuse me, sir/ma'am. How do you feel now? Are you still feeling bad?

SP : Yes .. (Groaning)

A : There will be an ambulance waiting at the airport. An airport medical team will move you to a hospital in the ambulance. We'll be doing everything to help you.

SP : Okay.

Substitution Drill 12-3-1

Direction : Practice the conversation with your partner using the information given in the table below.

A : Excuse me, sir/ma'am. How do you feel now? Are you still feeling bad?

SP : Yes .. (Groaning)

A : (1) _____ . (2) _____ .

We'll be doing everything to help you.

SP : Okay.

	(1) Follow-up measure 1	(2) Follow-up measure 2
A	There will be a medical team at the gate	They will take you to a hospital near the airport
B	A doctor will be waiting for you at the gate	He and his medical team will provide you with the proper treatment.
C	A medic will offer you treatment at the airport	He and his team will take you to a hospital

Dialogue 12-3-2   Track 63

Ensuring a pleasant atmosphere in the cabin during/after a medical emergency.

P : Passenger   A : Flight Attendant

P : Excuse me, miss. A doctor was paged a little while ago. What's going on?

A : We've had a medical emergency on board. Fortunately there is a doctor on board. He/She was able to assist.

P : Are we going to make an emergency landing?

A : No, we aren't. The passenger is fine and we'll be landing at our destination airport as planned.

P : I'm glad to hear that the passenger is fine.

A : He/She'll be fine. Thank you very much for your concern and cooperation.

Substitution Drill 12-3-2

Direction : Practice the conversation with your partner using the information given in the table below.

P : Excuse me, miss. (1) _____. What's going on?

A : We've had a medical emergency on board. Fortunately there is

(2) _____ on board. He/She was able to assist.

P : Are we going to make an emergency landing?

A : No, we aren't. (3) _____ and we'll be landing at

our destination airport as planned.

P : I'm glad to hear that the passenger is fine.

A : He/She'll be fine. Thank you very much for your concern and cooperation.

	(1) Paging	(2) Medical personnel	(3) Condition of the sick passenger
A	You were looking for a person with medical training	a nurse	The patient is getting better
B	You asked for a doctor or a nurse	a surgeon	His bleeding stopped
C	You were paging for a doctor or a person with medical training	a doctor	The patient is asleep and doing fine

사진
출처

5p.

Picture 1.   http://www.koreatowndaily.com/read.php?id=20080707180
236&section=local&type=fdb&ss=1&page=140

10p.

Picture 11.   http://www.aerospaceweb.org/aircraft/jetliner/b787/pics02.
shtml

11p.

Picture 13.   http://blog.koreanair.com/731
Picture 14.   http://bibletour.tistory.com/167
http://www.greentour.co.kr/info/08_1.html
Picture 15.   http://www.consumerpost.co.kr/news/articleView.html?idx
no=26320
http://cyberskyshop.koreanair.com/

27p.

Picture 1.   http://asia.etbtravelnews.com/154338/game-changing-a380-
flights-asia-start-sep-1st/

30p.

Picture 2.   http://www.flyasiana.com

31p.

Picture 3.   http://naringulec.wordpress.com/2011/03/23/boarding-pass-
re-design/
http://www.ausbt.com.au/should-airlines-redesign-your-
boar ding-pass-to-look-like-this

http://commons.wikimedia.org/wiki/File:Japan_Airlines_boarding_pass.jpg
http://blog.timoni.org/post/318322031/a-practical-boarding-pass-redesign

35p.

Picture 4. http://blog.koreanair.com/108

43p.

Picture 1. http://www.ausbt.com.au/united-upgrades-airbus-fleet-new-seats-larger-luggage-bins-wifi
Picture 2. http://www.pinterest.com/eirediva1/beauty-and-elegance-emirates-cabin-crew/

52p.

Picture 3. http://kr.koreanair.com/content/koreanair/korea/ko/traveling/services1.html#special-assistance
Picture 4. http:// idols2.dothome.co.kr/xe/a_1/411

54p.

Picture 5. http://m.mt.co.kr/renew/view.html?no=2006041911451122547

73p.

Picture 1. http://kr.koreanair.com/content/dam/koreanair/en/documents/BaggageServices/Prohibited%20Item%20List_en.pdf

79p.

Picture 1. http:// www.amazon.co.uk/Cocktail-Martini-Bartender-Bartending-Shaker/dp/B00BTA1YR8
Picture 2. http://businessnews.chosun.com/site/data/img_dir/2009/04/01/2009040100152_1.jpg

82p.

Picture 3. http://www.etoday.co.kr/news/section/newsview.php?idxno=430163

86p.

Picture 4. http://onemileatatime.boardingarea.com/2015/03/11/the-5-most-amazing-airbus-a380-amenities/

88p.

Picture 5. http://blog.koreanair.com/108

90p.

Picture 6. http://cphoto.asiae.co.kr/listimglink/6/2014082910444384226_1.jpg

92p.

Picture 7. http://cfile10.uf.tistory.com/image/2675DF4853C620E1306391

102p.

Picture 3. http://www.airliners.net/aviation-forums/trip_reports/read.main/153998/

106p.

Picture 5. http://dc.koreatimes.com/article/742172

114P.

Picture 2. http://www.luxuo.com/aircraft/inside-korean-air-airbus-a380.html

149p.

http://vishubs.tistory.com/5
http://uilove.egloos.com/m/3022712

150p.

http://www.ilbonuhak.com/info/ready.htm
http://airport.or.kr/airport/inout/depart_02_4_pop2.htm

186p.

http://www.qatarairways.com/docs/IFDF-order-form.pdf

232p.

Picture 1. http://cabincrewphotos.blogspot.kr/2012/02/air-china-stew-
ardess-training-program.html

233p.

Picture 2. http://www.astronics.com/products/aircraft-safety/first-aid-
kits.asp

Picture 3. http://www.statkit.com/statkit650

234p.

Picture 4. http://www.cocprassn.com/classes/heartsaver-all-ages-cpr-
and-aed-only/

Reference 참고문헌

Asiana Airlines Homepage

Korean Air Homepage

국가직무능력표준 홈페이지 :

      http://www.ncs.go.kr/ncs/page.do?sk=P1A2_PG01_001

저자소개

최경희

학력

학사 : 이화여자대학교 영어영문학

석사 : 캐나다 Carleton University 응용언어학

박사 : 고려대학교 영어영문학 (영어학 전공)

경력

(전) KBS 국제방송 영어방송 PD 겸 아나운서

(현) 한양여자대학교 항공과 교수

윤선정

학력

박사 : 경희대학교 호텔관광학

경력

(전) 아시아나항공

(현) 한양여자대학교 항공과 교수

항공객실서비스영어

초판 1쇄 발행 2016년 12월 15일
2판 1쇄 발행 2021년 2월 10일

저   자 최경희 ·윤선정

펴 낸 이 임 순 재

펴 낸 곳 (주)한올출판사

등   록 제11-403호

주   소 서울시 마포구 모래내로 83(성산동, 한올빌딩 3층)

전   화 (02)376-4298(대표)

팩   스 (02)302-8073

홈 페 이 지 www.hanol.co.kr

e - 메 일 hanol@hanol.co.kr

ISBN 979-11-6647-039-4